The New Knowledge

of

DOG BEHAVIOR

by Clarence J. Pfaffenberger

Foreword by Dr. J. P. Scott
Roscoe B. Jackson Memorial Laboratory
Bar Harbor, Maine

Consultant on Genetics:

Dr. Benson E. Ginsburg
Professor of Biology, University of Chicago

1985—Nineteenth Printing

HOWELL BOOK HOUSE INC.
230 Park Avenue
New York, N.Y. 10169

This is a revised, expanded and updated bound edition of a series of articles which appeared in PURE-BRED DOGS, *the American Kennel* GAZETTE, under the title of "Science Has a New Look at Behavior."

I wish to dedicate this book to

JUANITA

I am sure that few other men have been blessed with
a wife like mine who so thoroughly understood the importance of their hobbies to their well-being of mind
and body and who so unselfishly gave up many of her
own pleasures to help him realize so complete a ful-
fillment of his avocation.

Table of Contents

Foreword

Clarence Pfaffenberger is a man with the special gift of combining effective practical work with dogs with an appreciation of the value of basic scientific research. The result, as he describes it in this book, is that he has been able to set up a first-rate organization for the production of guide dogs and at the same time keep records which are of unusual scientific value and general interest.

One of the limitations of laboratory research is that while we are able to control the environment very accurately and so discover some of the unknown and little appreciated causes of behavior, our very accuracy makes the situation into an artificial one. Clarence Pfaffenberger's guide dogs go out into real life and thus provide the acid test of the theories which we work out in the laboratory.

In this book he tells the story of his work at Guide Dogs for The Blind, an organization which has in its own way made as great a contribution to this work as the pioneer institutions at Fortunate Fields and The Seeing Eye. He also tells of the many years of fruitful collaboration with workers at our Behavior Research Laboratory at Hamilton Station, and translates the resulting technical information into practical advice which every dog owner should have. I can recommend his book as being not only extremely readable but one which includes accurate and dependable information. At the same time, this taste of what scientific research can do whets our appetite for more. Man's best friend, and the oldest domesticated animal, is still in many ways a scientific mystery.

J. P. SCOTT
Roscoe B. Jackson Memorial Laboratory
Bar Harbor, Maine

Preface

The New Knowledge of Dog Behavior

Primarily, THE NEW KNOWLEDGE OF DOG BEHAVIOR is a story of how I, as a member of the Board of Directors of Guide Dogs for the Blind, Inc., San Rafael, California, set out to find the ideal puppy. To us the ideal puppy is one who, when he is about twelve months of age, will learn the lessons we teach him so well that his blind master or mistress will be perfectly safe in his care.

This is a story of how I was assigned to the task of finding the ideal puppy, who would become the ideal Guide Dog. The story tells how, with the help of a great many people across the entire United States, we have found how to breed and raise the almost ideal puppy.

Many ideas about dogs, which have always been accepted as true, have been exploded by research in the last fifteen years.

To me, there is a certain irony in the fact that science had to turn to the dog, man's best friend, to understand our own behavior better. What have we done to our children that we have created such a crop of persons who are mentally ill, criminal, or delinquent?

This book will not attempt to evaluate the scientific findings in human values, but it will tell some of the things to do, and when to do them, to prevent similar developments in our dogs.

Results speak for themselves. Fourteen years ago we found that only nine per cent of the dogs who were started in training for Guide Dogs at our school could be trained to become responsible Guides. In 1958 and in 1959 all the dogs who had been bred and developed by the new knowledge were as good or better than the best dogs we graduated in 1946. Even with our much stricter requirements, 90% became Guide Dogs.

It was our good fortune that Dr. J. Paul Scott had started a study of puppies to learn about children at Bar Harbor, Maine, the year prior to my assignment, and that I met him and his associates who have given us so much wonderful help.

Introduction

The dog family, to me, is the most interesting family in all animal life outside the family of man himself. In many ways he is much like man, so much so that we can sometimes study our own behavior best by studying the behavior of dogs, especially puppies. This is true because a dog's behavior toward his human family (owners) is so much like that of a child toward his own family. A puppy's behavior toward his own mother, and her behavior toward him, are very similar to the child's behavior toward his mother and the human mother's behavior toward her child.

Our similarities have made it possible for man and dog to live together for many thousands of years, and it is these similarities that make a study of dogs' behavior so valuable in the study of human behavior.

But it is our dissimilarities which have brought man and dog together and kept them together as a team so very long. Because we are dissimilar we complement each other's abilities. Thus, these dissimilarities have worked to the benefit of both man and dog. Because a dog is willing, even eager, to assist man, his ability to do things we cannot do (or, if we can do them, to do them better than man can) has enabled man to use a dog's capabilities as a projection of his own, or, in the case of a Guide Dog, to substitute for an ability he has lost.

Dogs vary in ability and appearance more than any other species of animal. This, too, makes them especially suitable for study because it offers the student such a wide range of character traits and physical traits to study. Some of these differences probably came about by mutation over many thousands of years. Some have come about by the climate in which dogs live, such as the Northern Dogs who have a large, well-feathered curly tail with which they can cover their nose and eyes when they lie down in the snow and thus keep from freezing. Many have been man-made by selective breeding. Man has found that a certain character trait or physical trait has proven to be more useful to

In 1946 the School purchased 11½ acres near San Rafael, California. On this acreage has been built one of the finest Guide Dog schools in the world. It was here that we set about our serious search for the perfect puppy.

him for the particular type of work he wished his canine companion to do for him, and so he has kept the puppies which showed they had these traits. By breeding these together he has produced dogs which look very different from any other dog, and who have greater abilities in certain types of work than other dogs. Some may have been developed, too, as they are, simply because a certain man or group of men admired certain characteristics in their dogs. Man and his dog, having spread to all parts of the world, also developed differently because they became separated from others of their kind. But the general behavior characteristic of each species has persisted in all different races and breeds.

While man has developed some of the dog's potentials, it is evident to anyone who works with dogs seriously that he has not nearly approached the use of a dog's full potentiality. This is not surprising since most of us have come to understand that man had never yet understood his own potentiality, or in any way nearly achieved it.

Good examples of the different effects which selection has produced are evident in two very different breeds: the Pekingese and the greyhound. It is said that at one time the Pekingese was one of the largest and fiercest breeds. As the favorite of Chinese rulers, it became a royal household pet. Its aggressiveness, to the extent that it has no fear, was preserved, but its size and physical equipment for combat were bred out. This may have been done intentionally, or it may have come about through intense inbreeding and the selection of the smaller, more manageable dogs for breeding stock. I do not believe that anyone knows for sure whether the owners purposely reduced the size and defense abilities, or the selection and inbreeding simply happened because the dogs were restricted to such a small number that, once characteristics were set, they became definitely fixed.

The greyhound, on the other hand, must have been quite deliberately developed for his ability to pursue game. All his close relatives, like him, come from wide open countries where a fleet-footed dog is of great value in running down antelope and other fleet meat animals. It would be natural for the wild ancestors to develop the same physical and character traits, yet

9

the greyhound and his cousins, the Afghan and Saluki, show the handiwork of intelligent selective breeding by their original breeders, just as the Arabian horses show the mastery of this same science.

We have more than one hundred breeds which are recognized as distinct and separate by leading kennel clubs. Even though these may be bunched in six groups which represent to a certain degree general family traits, or in some cases uses for which the dogs are bred, they are all definitely distinct. Still, all of them, no matter how different in appearance, have basically the same natural social behavior which they inherited from their wild, wolf-like ancestors. Each of them has retained certain basic inherited traits which makes him susceptible to environmental influences at certain definite periods in his life.

No matter how different they are in appearance, how completely unalike they are in physical structure, when the breeds meet they recognize each other as dogs. All varieties will interbreed, even with wolves, and the mating will produce dog offspring who are fertile when bred to other dogs. To me this would seem to indicate that most of the changes from the wild dog ancestor to the many shapes and sizes and intelligences and temperaments have been brought about very largely, if not entirely, by selective breeding, either purposefully employed by intelligent owners or through accidental selection by others.

Dogs retain another trait from their wild ancestors which we have recognized as very important only recently; that is, the natural tendency to form a pack.

It is this instinct to "pack," or to remain in a cooperative family group, that has made it possible for man and dog to live and work so effectively together. On the surface it seems phenomenal that, given the opportunity at the right time to make a choice, a dog will prefer to associate himself with a human family rather than with a dog family. Actually, certain specific time elements and environmental conditions are necessary or this phenomenon does not take place. But if it does, the dog brings with him the "pack" social behavior trait which makes possible his ability to cooperate in achievements both with other dogs and with man. This makes it possible, though they have inherited this together with other social behavior traits from wild ancestors, for man to mold dog behavior to suit his needs and to fit into his family life.

Dogs still have a very great ability to adapt themselves to the changing conditions which modern man experiences and yet, in primitive lands, dogs still fit in with the environments and the social patterns of their masters. Almost everywhere that man has been found, dogs have been with him and have adapted to his needs of the time and place in which he lived. No animal has associated with man as long as the dog. No other animal voluntarily associates with man in preference to his own kind.

Many animals can be taught to do certain routines in helping man, but only the dog shows such great joy in learning and in working with mankind. It is because we have never before understood why this is true that our dogs have not reached an even higher plane of service to mankind. We have not known before when and how to tap the sources of their ability. Now that this is known we should develop very superior dogs. (If it happens, as it very likely will, that a similar situation exists in our approach to human behavior, great progress may be made from these discoveries.) While I am not qualified to evaluate the meaning of these findings in terms of future human behavior, scientists with whom I have worked are so qualified, and it is their belief that these findings will be of great value in human social progress.

Like men, dogs are happiest when they are doing something worthwhile. We find this to be especially true in Guide Dogs for the Blind. You can inflict no greater cruelty on one of them than to separate him from his master and his work. Praise and the joy of accomplishment are the only rewards they receive; the joy of doing something for the men and women they serve which their owners cannot do for themselves. They are as joyful when they see their master pick up their harness as your hunting dog is when he sees you take your gun from the rack. They are as attentive to commands as a sheepdog is to those of a shepherd. In addition to all this, they take the responsibility of deciding whether what the master wishes them to do is safe or unsafe. If it is not safe, the master yields to the dog's decision.

11

To man or dog, child or puppy, the greatest deterrent to supreme happiness is ennui: boredom resulting from a lack of something to do. This is what prevents dogs from achieving their greatest potential.

Puppies start to learn at three weeks of age. From seven weeks to sixteen weeks of age they are going to learn the things which will mold their character as adults. If they are not taught by their human masters, they will find a way to learn other things on their own. This is one of the great discoveries which has completely revolutionized the raising and training of Guide Dog puppies, with remarkable results. How all this was learned is a part of this story.

While all dogs inherit their natural social behaviors and certain physical and character traits, the selection for specialized work through the centuries has accentuated certain character traits, just as it has accentuated certain physical appearances and abilities. In a general way these are usually associated with breeds. But dogs have individualities just as we have. They have individual abilities which are inherited. Thus, an accumulation of these abilities in a particular strain or family can make that family outstanding in certain fields of activity. Owners of field trial dogs, herding dogs and racing dogs, for example, try to accumulate these special traits for each type of activity in their strains.

In work such as leading the blind, a very special dog is needed and the selection and accumulation of genes which produce that dog are of great importance. Because it is so important to produce these very special dogs, we at Guide Dogs for the Blind, Inc., in San Rafael, California, have devoted fourteen years to research. What we have learned, where and how we have learned it, and how we are using what we have learned, is told in this book.

Since I am not a scientist but a practical dog breeder, I have been extremely fortunate to have the assistance of the leading men in the field of animal behavior, and access to their complete research. We have worked together searching for new knowledge, and have been fortunate to have made some very significant findings. While I am not a scientist, my practical experience has been of such a nature that it may be of interest to you. You have a right to know with what authority I speak and why I have come to the conclusions which I have. All parts of the book which refer to studies made at Roscoe B. Jackson Memorial Laboratory, Animal Behavior Division, Bar Harbor, Maine, have been read and approved by the scientists whose names are used in connection with the experiments and conclusions.

Ten chapters of this book, more or less as it appears here, were published in *Pure-Bred Dogs*, the American Kennel Club magazine, and I wish to acknowledge here with thanks the permission granted by their editor, Mr. Arthur Frederick Jones, to use these in whole or in part.

Our study has brought about a new concept in how puppies should be raised and trained. Selection of both the best dogs for training and for breeding can be made through aptitude tests we have developed, if given before thirteen weeks of age. We have also learned how to hoard the genes which transmit some of the desirable traits. We are exploring ways of selecting and hoarding more. We are at present exploring the ways to avoid disease and malformations which have troubled all dog breeders. Leading veterinarians and anatomists are aiding us in this program.

The scientists at Bar Harbor are studying puppies to find out why WE behave the way WE do. What we have gained from their studies is a very valuable by-product. It is helping us to develop better dogs to lead the blind people of our country. A reader who is not interested in dogs per se may still be interested to know what both the Bar Harbor and the San Rafael studies reveal. Ironically, San Rafael has found some new knowledge which may be very important to those who are studying the human race and its foibles.

At Guide Dogs for the Blind, Inc., the blind students do not receive their dogs until the fourth day after they arrive at the school. An instructor takes the place of the dog for the first three days. He holds the leash, later the harness, and obeys the commands just as the dog will obey them later when the student learns exactly how to give commands and knows what to expect when he gives them. In this picture Larry Rees, Director of Training, is taking the part of a Guide Dog. In this chapter the author has taken the place of a dog to illustrate how character traits are inherited and how environment affects our lives.

CHAPTER I

What We Can Learn From a Pedigree

I had set out to find out how to produce an ideal Guide Dog.

Once you have found out how to produce the thing you want, the next step is to know how to produce more, equally good products—in my case, other dogs as good as the ideal dog, if not exactly like the ideal dog.

In all nature there are no two men, animals, or plants exactly alike. The more we work with nature the more we come to see that this is true, and learn that nature, through genetic inheritance, has made this automatic. If this were not true there would be little or no improvement in nature. All life would become static. Once a pattern was set it would become a mold, and succeeding generations would be identical. There would be no evolution. There would be no improvement. There would be no progress.

The word "individual" applies to a person, an animal or a plant, and means just that: a distinctly different being. As individuals we are less distinct from our relatives than we are from non-relatives. This is because we have the same, or partly the same, pedigree as our relatives, according to our relationship. The same applies to animals and plants.

Our pedigree is a sort of genetic recipe which details the ingredients from which we were made. No matter how closely we are related, however, we never are exactly alike, and neither

15

are animals or plants. The same recipe combining genes from two parents always produces offspring with some degree of difference. This is because of the way the genes are combined, and because there are so many genes that there is no likelihood that the same combination will ever take place twice. The reason for this is that no one ever inherits all of his genes from one parent. Half of our genes come from our father and half from our mother, and the other half from each is discarded at the time of conception and has no bearing upon what we are to become.

Because there are so many genes, and almost any half from one parent can combine with any half from the other parent, brothers and sister can be very different and litter mates can vary greatly in physical, emotional and mental character traits. The degree to which they can vary will depend upon the degree the parents were different or alike. In studying a pedigree, then, we look at the parents and determine as best we can the likenesses and the differences, the strengths and the weaknesses, of the parents.

Because we understand people better than animals I shall use my own pedigree to help explain how we use the pedigree of a dog. I think it will make our study easier just as it has made my understanding of dogs easier to put myself in their place at times.

At Guide Dogs for the Blind, Inc., our instructors take each blind student and explain to him each piece of equipment he will use with his Guide Dog. The collar is studied, and the manner in which it should be used is explained. The special leash, which can be made into different lengths for different uses, is carefully examined by the student; how to change it and how to use it are explained. The harness that is used to lead the blind person is carefully examined and explained. The commands which a blind person gives his dog, and the things the dog will do when he has been given one of these commands, are explained.

But this is not all. The instructor then acts as the dog. Working at the opposite end of the leash from the student, he has the student give him commands, which he executes as if he were the dog until the student is letter perfect. The student then has the same training with the harness, the instructor acting as the dog while they learn to go in and out of doors, up and down stairs, around obstacles, turn at corners, cross streets, and get into vehicles. By the third day the student is usually ready to work with his dog.

Now let us return to our study of pedigrees.

The father and mother are the most important parts of any pedigree because half of the genes, which make us what we are, come from each parent. I shall use the maiden names of the wives to avoid undue length in the human pedigrees.

In the formalized diagram which is used for pedigrees, the individual always appears on the left and the ancestors are arranged in columns from left to right according to the relationship.

Newton J. Pfaffenberger
(father)

Clarence J. Pfaffenberger

Anna Louisa Meyer
(mother)

One of our most valuable dogs at Guide Dogs for the Blind, Inc., would have a simple pedigree.

Frank of Ledge Acres
(sire)

Guide Dogs' Odin

Guide Dogs' Olivia
(dam)

Because we inherit every physical, mental, temperamental, and emotional trait from our parents we find it very important to know everything we can learn about each parent. Everything that we are born with we inherit from our parents; nothing that ever happens in our life will add to or take away from what we inherited, unless it is removed by surgery. Environment will modify, but never add nor take away.

Despite the fact that environment has a profound effect on every living thing and modifies the manner in which inherited traits are used, only what we inherit determines what we can be. Environment has never made a man, animal or plant any better than the genes he or it inherited. What is often referred to as an

17

"ideal climate" can help any individual achieve his potential or nearly his potential. Poor environment can cripple the development of an individual until he can never achieve the potential he was born with, even if an ideal climate is later provided.

It is important to remember this because, when we look at an individual and his achievements, we should take into consideration whether he or she had an opportunity to develop into the individual that he or she could be, or if some adverse conditions handicapped the full development, whether physical, mental, temperamental, or emotional. That is where environment comes in; it will be studied later.

When we started to try to develop an ideal Guide Dog, we had two other means of selecting the ancestors from which to try to produce this dog. One was by trial and error—the mating of two dogs and studying the offspring to determine whether they would produce the kind of individuals we were looking for. This we did and, at first, if we found a mating that would produce one puppy who would become a good Guide Dog out of an entire litter we were happy. Nowadays we are unhappy with a litter in which even one dog fails to make a Guide Dog. That is how important it is to know what your pedigree means and how to use it.

Our other means of selection was to study the grandparents. We were interested in obtaining genes which had produced individuals who were willing to do things for people. When we studied Odin's grandparents we began to hope that here we had some indications that these traits would be inherited.

Here is his extended pedigree:

Vosefeld's Arras C.D.X.

Frank of Ledge Acres

Helen of Ledge Acres

Guide Dogs' Odin

Orkos of Longworth UDT

Guide Dogs' Olivia

Guide Dogs' Doris

These grandparents seemed to indicate that they were willing to do things for people. At least the two grandfathers had been

18

successfully trained in obedience and acquired titles. The C.D.X. following the name of Vosefeld's Arras indicates that he was made a Companion Dog Excellent, having qualified in three separate obedience trials for Companion Dog and three additional, more severe test for Companion Dog Excellent. In the case of Orkos, he had gone two steps farther and acquired not only the titles of Companion Dog and Companion Dog Excellent, but also the much more difficult to obtain titles of Utility Dog and Tracking Dog.

In addition to this, Orkos had a great record as a War Dog in World War II. In fact, it is our information that Orkos was the first German Shepherd in the United States to have won his UDT. In theory Arras and Orkos each contributed one fourth of the genes which determined what Odin would be. Together they contributed half. If Odin inherited their obedient, willing genes he would have valuable genes to contribute to building the kind of family that would make Ideal Guide Dogs.

There was more in this pedigree. The father of Orkos was from Fortunate Field, the original guide dog school. The father of Doris was also a C.D.X. dog. What is more, all six ancestors shown in this abbreviated pedigree approached our ideal.

It is interesting to study our own pedigrees and ancestors to see how much they have affected our own lives. It helps, I think, to put into better perspective what we may expect to accomplish through the use of dog pedigrees.

According to our family tree the first Pfaffenberger was so named because he was the Pope's Chamberlain in Vienna. Our family record shows that our great grandparents Pfaffenberger had been Methodists who migrated from Bavaria to settle government land in Southern Indiana. These two ancestors contributed one eighth each to the genes which I inherited. Their son, my grandfather, inherited half of his genes from each; my father inherited half his genes from my grandfather; I inherited my genes from my own parents, half from one and half from the other.

Let us see what happens if we go back and start with those eighths we inherit from each great grandparent.

19

My great great grandparents Pfaffenberger settled on government land and, having been frugal farmers in Bavaria, they began to cut down and burn the hardwood forests which covered their land and to cultivate corn and wheat and hay. They had several sons and a daughter. All of the sons but one married nice German girls from the neighboring German families and settled down to developing fine farms and sending their children to college to become Methodist ministers, school teachers, and newspaper men. The daughter married a merchant and one of her boys became a merchant, and another a newspaper man, and the third a school superintendent. The merchant's son became a newspaper man.

Did these genes which influenced so many to choose fields of self-expression come from our ancient ancestor, the Pope's Chamberlain? He must have had some way of gaining recognition or he would never have been chosen for so important a position. None of us ever heard of our great grandparents' having any special interest in self-expression by writing or speaking. In fact, Great Grandfather Pfaffenberger financed his family and farm, until he got the farm paying, by making shoes for all the families in the neighborhood; the merchant grandson was the owner of the Bush Shoe Store in Seymour, Indiana.

My grandfather was the only son to marry a non-German girl. He married the red-headed Cox girl who lived on the adjoining farm. The Cox farm was as different from the Pfaffenberger farms as the Coxes were different from the Pfaffenbergers. On the Pfaffenberger farms the land was cleared and crops were grown to the capacity of the land's potential. On the Cox farm there was no need to grub stumps or plow around them; there was only the underbrush to be cut. Grass was sown in the open places, the streams were kept clear, and a stock-tight fence enclosed the entire one hundred sixty acres. On this natural growth of grass, browse and mast, some of the finest gaited horses, work oxen, and fat hogs were raised for the market. The farmers came from miles to buy a saddle horse, a yoke of oxen, or fine hogs. My Great Grandfather Cox rode over his fields and mended his fences, hunted Bob White with a good setter and smiled at the German neighbors grubbing for a living while his grew quite naturally. From Kentucky, where he was born, he had brought a fine Jack and soon the German neighbors were changing some of their farming from ox-drawn to mule-drawn implements, drawn by the mules sired by this Jack.

The Cox family had originated in Wales, where they were called Coaxxe. In their migrations they first stopped for a generation in Edinburgh, Scotland, where the name was changed to Cox. Irked with city life, they moved to Pennsylvania, then to Kentucky and finally to Indiana. Somewhere along the way my great grandfather met and married the Williams girl whose family had come directly from Wales to the United States. They were both happy with live stock and nature and all the children showed a tendency toward these things. My grandmother was the only one of the five Cox girls to marry into a German family. She, however, maintained some of her old life of having good live stock, especially a saddle horse of her own, and a good dog. My father was her only son. He had two sisters, each of whom married and moved to cities and seemed perfectly happy with city life.

When my father was twenty-two years old he had a pair of gaited saddle horses and some good work stock. He rented some White River bottom land near Brownstown, Indiana, to raise corn and hogs. Here he met Annie Louisa Meyer. "She was the most wonderful girl I had ever seen," he often told me. They were married and, sixty-six years later, he still felt the same way as she sat holding his hand as he breathed his last. I was the fifth of twelve children, eight boys and four girls. Six of us are still alive, four boys and two girls. Of the six of us, two have taught school and two have shown a special interest in animals, especially dogs. I taught school for twenty-eight and a half years, was employed on newspapers for ten years, and in kindred fields another ten years. During the time I taught school I taught journalism.

For twenty-five years I have been interested in dogs as a hobby. During the last fourteen years I have been engaged in serious research concerning dogs. Ever since I can remember, I have been interested in dogs, and, I've been told, I was interested in them before I can remember.

Did I inherit this aptitude? Science shows that all our aptitudes are inherited. Our skills develop through use or practice, and the ability to employ an aptitude may be accelerated by an environment which provides a proper opportunity.

In the opposite manner an environment may suppress or bury a natural aptitude so completely that it never becomes evident. It has been found by studying puppies that there are times very early in his life when he needs these opportunities to develop his aptitudes, especially those aptitudes which have to do with social behavior and cooperation, or he will never be nearly as good a dog as he could have been. We will soon come to environment. Let us now look at the other side, or the bottom part, of my pedigree.

Both my grandfather and my grandmother, Meyer, were born and raised in Hanover. Grandpa's mother was a widow and shared a duplex house with Widow Uphouse. While they were small, grandpa and John Uphouse, who were about the same age, took the village cows, sheep, and geese to the commons and tended them each summer to supplement their mothers' incomes; they grew up with a love for nature and animals, and became almost like brothers.

When grandpa came home from the Civil War with "galloping consumption," no doctor could tell him what to do to save his life. A quack told him that if he would kill and eat his pet dog he would get well. He and grandma in desperation decided to try it. My ninety-pound grandmother butchered the dog while tears froze on her cheeks. Then she tried to prepare it so he would not suspect, being as cheerful as she could. He never ate a bite, nor could he eat any other food for days, for he suspected what she had done, and so they both cried over the loss of their beloved dog to no avail.

When my father and mother were married my grandmother, who had been named executor of the estate, divided the land among the children. Mama's land was better suited for pasture, hay and small grain, so papa continued to farm corn in the White River bottom. This gave him an ideal set-up for live stock breeding. He started with horses and mules while using feeder cattle and hogs to help finance the type of farming he preferred.

One day he had a chance to buy a well trained black-and-white setter like the one his mother had had. There were lots of bobwhite on both places. He could have gotten a farm-dog pup from a neighbor free, but having hunted with his grandfather's and his mother's dogs he had to have that dog; although it cost him about what he would have to pay a farm hand for two months' work, he bought it. The price was $35.00. My parents moved to Colorado when I was one and a half years old. I am told that I was very fond of the setter, but I do not remember her. Transportation of dogs in those days was next to impossible for so great a distance, so my father sold the setter at a profit, but he often told me of her prowess. Even in his old age papa would say to me, "Clarence, I never felt so badly about parting with any animal as I did about selling that setter."

If we study the ancestors of any individual, man or dog, for evidence that they possessed the traits which are most important to achieve a purpose or to fit into a pattern that will be valuable, we have a much better chance that any predictions we make of traits the individual will inherit will be fairly reliable. We can also, in a dog breeding program, usually avoid bringing together two parents who have traits which are unsuitable for our purpose. This is where a pedigree is useful, if we know more about it than just the names which appear upon it. If you know that one parent has some undesirable trait, but the dog has other qualities so important that you want them, selection of a mate without the bad trait will help to breed it out. But you will have to be alert and firm in eliminating all those who do inherit the bad trait until it has disappeared completely; this may take three or four generations, and can best be done by inbreeding.

Inbreeding is so controversial among dog breeders that we will not attempt to show why we use it here, but we will show you how. Why is explained in detail in the study of the descendants of Frank of Ledge Acres in another chapter. Our inbreeding is done by strains. In our German shepherds we have three strains: Frankie, Odin and Orkos. Odin is a Frankie son and an Orkos grandson, so, when his strain is out crossed to either Frankie or Orkos strain, the resulting puppies are still in the Frankie or Orkos line, but are not necessarily inbred.

23

It is common practice to speak of a dog's bloodline. This is incorrect. Blood has nothing to do with it. The genes are what count. So we have set up gene banks of Frankie, Odin and Orkos genes by keeping descendants of them and breeding them together. The original dogs are all gone, but today we are making a mating which will give us as many of Frankie's genes in the puppies as if he were the sire and the bitch were his daughter or twelve-sixteenths Frankie. This is true even though the first place Frankie appears on the pedigree is as great grandfather of the puppies-to-be.

This form of hoarding the genes of an outstanding individual seems to be working very well. If it continues to prove as satisfactory as it has to date it will provide all dog people with a method of preserving the fine traits of any dog they greatly admire almost indefinitely, and almost in the form in which they were admired. We call this form of hoarding "Gene Banks." We have worked out a form which we call the "San Rafael Pedigree," which aids us in studying the character traits, physical traits, and gene inheritance of all our breeding stock, approximately ninety dogs. We will illustrate with the use of a planned breeding of Odin (while he was still alive) to Fashion. Odin = 8/16 Frankie, Fashion = 12/16 Frankie, puppies = 10/16 Frankie.

So, in addition to the use of trial and error breeding, to be sure of which will make the best breeding combinations we use the known traits of the ancestors and, by combining the ancestors who had the best traits and preserving those traits in our gene banks, we have a far greater control of the results than we could otherwise have. We also now have the advantage of aptitude test records on nearly all of our breeding stock. In some cases this goes back to as many as a dozen ancestors. In the San Rafael Pedigree below, this plays an important part. The grades are 0 for failure, 1 border-line, 2 and 3 passing, 4 and 5 superior. The tests are small experiences in the life of a Guide Dog, given to puppies from eight to twelve weeks of age. We use them with confidence both in selecting Guides and breeding stock.

24

THE SAN RAFAEL PEDIGREE

Puppy Test Scores for	Odin	Fashion	Probable Litter's Scores
Come	3	5	4
Sit	4	4	4
Fetch	3	4	3
Heel	4	4	4
Closeness	4	5	4
Crossings	4	4	4
Traffic Check	4	4	4
Body Sensitivity	4	5	4
Ear Sensitivity	4	5	4
Intelligent Response	4	4	4
Willing Temperament	4	4	4
Pelvic X-ray	5	4	4
Height Metric	540	585	560 = 23.5 Inches
Weight Metric	333	294	310 = 68 Lbs.

What we actually have here, since this is inbreeding, is an expectancy of nothing in the litter less than this very desirable score. Many should make scores equal to the best of either parent. It is quite conceivable that one or two might have nothing less than a 4 and also have the four 5's from Fashion and the one 5 from Odin. Such a pup would be carefully raised for breeding.

By being your dog for a while, I hope I brought home how dogs inherit traits which shape the potential of their usefulness, and in what field, just as humans inherit traits and tendencies toward certain fields of self expression.

The other thing that shapes our life is environment. It is important to remember that, no matter how much the environment may present a wonderful opportunity, neither man nor dog will take maximum advantage of it if he has not inherited traits which make this opportunity seem desirable to him. In studying ancestors for the desirable traits we are searching for in the future generations, we must know whether the ancestor ever had an opportunity to use the trait for which we are searching, or we must have some device like our aptitude tests which reveal whether or not a descendant has inherited the traits.

One thing we must keep in mind is that environment never has given man or dog any ability he did not inherit. Environment either provides the opportunity for complete fruition of the inherited abilities or it limits their development even to the extent of complete frustration. As an example, a man whom I know had a very promising eight-week-old cocker spaniel puppy. He placed her in the care of a very wonderful puppy field trial trainer. She became one of America's great Cocker Field Trial Champions. She was bred to a dog with equally good genes from the same strain. The litter of puppies was raised in a stall in a barn. Water and food were placed in the stall once or twice a week. No one was allowed to handle the puppies. At four months of age these puppies would try to bury themselves by digging if approached by anyone. In the field they hunted as if they had been well trained, naturally, but if anyone spoke to them they would lie flat on the ground and freeze as if paralyzed and their bodies felt as cold as if they were dead. A great deal of care was given these young dogs to try to socialize them, but only one ever became anything like a normal dog.

After we moved to Colorado we did not have a dog of our own for more than a year, but a neighbor, who had a son about my age, Maynard Porter, had a Labrador retriever named Box. Our mothers were great friends and so I got to play with Maynard and Box. One day we were having so much fun that our mothers came to investigate why all the mirth. Maynard had fallen into a small irrigation ditch and Box had jumped in and pulled him out. So that seemed like a nice game and Maynard pushed me in. Box pulled me out. This was still going on when our mothers arrived on the scene and removed our wet clothes and warmed our bare bottoms. I had to borrow a dress from Maynard to wear home. (Boys wore dresses at 2 years of age in 1891.) After that we had fun with Box by letting him retrieve things other than ourselves from the canals.

Maynard's older brother built a two-wheeled cart and rigged a harness so we could hitch Box up and one ride while the other led. I could hardly leave after each visit, I was so intrigued with Box.

Before I was born, infant diseases had taken my three older

26

brothers. My sister, Bertha, ten years older than I, did most of the housework so that mama could work in the fresh air with garden and poultry to improve her health. I think the loss of my three brothers had given me a special place in the family affection. Papa always took me everywhere with him, even on his lap when he was mowing hay. Once, when a tiny cottontail ran out ahead of the mower, he stopped and let me down to catch it. Then he unhitched early and we went to the barn where he built me a little hutch and showed me how to feed the rabbit on cow's milk by soaking the milk in a little piece of twisted cloth and letting the bunny nurse that. Once we found a half grown teal duck. We caught it and he showed me how to feed and care for it.

These animals were very interesting, but I could not play with them as I could with a dog. There were no quail in Colorado then, and I do not believe there were any setters. I do not remember ever seeing a setter until I was seventeen years old. There were a lot of spaniels and retrievers, for the Colorado river was a fly-way and lots of waterfowl passed that way. I guess papa still longed for a setter, but there were no bobwhite and no setters, so he did not get me a dog; not until after I had had a bad experience.

In November papa took me with him to the town hall, where he went to vote. Leaving me outside the booth while he voted gave me a chance to explore. I saw a big black-and-tan farm shepherd standing alone in the middle of the hall. I did not know that the dog belonged to a recluse who never spoke to anyone and did not allow his dog to be friendly. So when I went to stroke the dog's head he charged. When we left the doctor's office with five stitches in my face the experiment seemed to be a rather dismal failure, but it turned out quite well. At home papa took down his twelve-gauge shotgun and some shells.

"I have never killed a dog in my life," he said, "but I will not have a dog in the neighborhood who will bite a child."

"All you will do is cause a lot of hard feelings and maybe get yourself shot," my mother counseled. "We know how crazy Clarence is about dogs and he has always been with dogs who knew children. That dog had probably never had a child approach it before in its life. It would be much better if we would get Clarence a dog of his own so that he would not bother other people's dogs."

"That is a good idea," papa said, and put the gun back on the rack.

On April 25, 1892, I got my first pup as a birthday present. It was a three-month-old cocker spaniel. My father liked her because she reminded him somewhat of his setter, but he did not know until many years later, when I told him after just learning it myself, that setters, all breeds, are big spaniels and for many years were known as "setting spaniels."

From then on I always had one or more dogs until the years while I attended college, was in the army and traveled in Latin America. Even then I always felt the need for one.

The first few years after Juanita and I were married we talked about getting a dog but never got one. Then I was hospitalized because of old war injuries just after our older daughter Helenjoy was born and, while in the hospital, became friends with a fellow patient who was a breeder of Airedale Terriers. He insisted upon giving Helenjoy a puppy. That was a fine dog and my first experience with terriers. My health did not improve enough that I could return to my business, but fortunately the San Francisco school department offered me a teaching position in journalism. This called for a move to the city from Modesto. While getting adjusted we left our Airedale in Modesto and he was killed in an accident before we had a chance to move him. There was another lapse of five years before we had another dog.

My environment through childhood had been one in which I had become accustomed to having animals, especially dogs as companions. My father had fine horses and all were taught to work without a line. His mother had died when he was eight years old and he had gone to live with his Cox grandparents, where his employment had been to teach calves to haul wood, working in a yoke and minding "gee" and "haw." All his knowledge of dogs and horses and oxen he taught me from the time I was two years of age. He taught me where the rabbits hide, and all the ways of nature.

CHAPTER II

How Man and Dog Influence Each Other

The ideal Guide Dog, in addition to his expert ability to guide, has a special talent for companionship and a morale-building quality which gives that little extra boost to lift his owner out of the dumps, into which it is quite natural for a person without sight to fall. For this reason the instructors at Guide Dogs for the Blind, Inc., always train twelve dogs for a class of eight. This gives them flexibility in matching dogs with people so that the proper relationship will develop between the master and his dog.

Man and dogs were civilized together. An anthropologist or sociologist could pretty well classify any civilization if he had access to the dogs it owned. The dogs of the Christian countries are different from those of non-Christian. The dogs of the most advanced civilizations differ from those of the lower levels. Even in the Christian countries there is a great modification of the dogs, depending upon social and political attitudes and upon affluence and poverty. Dogs have the flexibility to adjust to the master's need. Through the ages their traits have become the kind which the particular people they serve need most. It is for this reason that a dog's association can become a definite therapeutic for his master's or mistress' illness.

These facts started to take definite form in the minds of Juanita and me more than twenty-five years ago as the result of an event which started in a doctor's office in San Francisco. Of course there were no dogs in the office. There were our five-year-old daughter, Kathleen, the doctor, her office nurse, Juanita and myself.

When the doctor had completed her examination of Kathleen she nodded to the nurse.

"Kathleen, let's you and me go into this room and look at the toys," the nurse suggested.

As they left the examination room, the doctor led Juanita and me into her private office. When we were all seated she said, "I am going to need your complete cooperation. Your daughter has a heart condition. It could be serious, but fortunately, I feel we have caught it in time. Whether we have or not will depend on what each of the three of us does during the next six months. All your plans for awhile will have to be made with this in mind. Kathleen needs every bit of help we can give her."

We had entered Kathleen in kindergarten as soon as she was old enough to attend, not realizing that, since her birthday was in April, she would not be old enough at the end of the term to be promoted to the first grade.

When she returned for a second term of kindergarten, the monotony of doing the same things she had done the term before, the frustration of being left behind her classmates, upset our little girl so much that she came home crying each day and begged not to be sent back to school. Although we were worried about Kathleen's condition when we consulted the child specialist, we certainly had not expected to be told that we had any problem as serious as this.

"I do not want Kathleen to go back to kindergarten at all. This was her last day. When her sister, Helenjoy, comes home from school let them play together, but avoid exciting games. Do not invite the neighbor children or any other friends in to play, and do not allow her to play out front with them.

"She will need a substitute for her child friends. I suggest that you buy her a pet, say, a puppy."

"Do you think that a nice cocker spaniel would be all right?" I asked. I had been lonesome for a cocker and could not resist putting words in the doctor's mouth.

"I think that a cocker spaniel would be just fine," she smiled, "but I have a special assignment for you." She looked me straight in the eye. "You can do one of the most important things that has to be done with this child.

"This little girl needs a lot of quiet and rest," she continued. "It is fortunate that you are a teacher and will have several weeks of summer vacation soon."

Then she explained how I could help.

The next weekend we took a leisurely trip to Juanita's parents' home in Modesto. Without telling Kathleen or Helenjoy our misssion, we set out to find the puppy for Kathleen. The first place we visited was the home of Mr. and Mrs. Jack Hunt. There, on an acre of lawn, romped two or three litters of cocker spaniel puppies together with half a dozen grown dogs. One little black female had found a piece of old blue shirt which she carried in her mouth as she dashed between the others, daring them to take it away from her. She caught our eye and soon she was ours.

Back in San Fransico, before the week was out Kathleen was hauling the puppy around in her little wagon in our back yard. When Helenjoy came home from school the two would dress Patsy up in doll clothes and push her around the yard in their doll buggy.

Now the part the doctor had given me to do had to be planned. It was fortunate for us that we had friends, Mr. and Mrs. William Swartz, who had a small resort in the Lassen National Forest. So, the next day after school was out, we packed for a summer in the mountains.

The first day we were there I found a place on Battle Creek which our friends had picked out for Kathleen and me. It was a small sand bar where a big pool formed above a pretty little water fall. Azaleas bloomed along the water's edge and hung over, shading the north bank. Above them, manzanita climbed toward the lava lip of the canyon and pines took over along the sunny slope. Upstream was a flowering buckeye in which birds nested. They entertained us by bringing mouthfuls of insects for the young to stretch their necks and open their big beaks to gobble down. Only a deserted logging road led to this spot.

The doctor had said, "I want you to take Kathleen and her

puppy to some quiet place where she can play and rest as she feels like it. I want you to do this all summer. Avoid all excitement. Read to her. Let her and her puppy romp as much as they wish, but do not encourage any exciting games. Leave right after breakfast. Take a good lunch along, but stay at your retreat until supper time. After supper Kathleen is to go to bed.''

Every day, all summer long, Kathleen, Patsy and I drove to our secluded spot. There were squirrels and chipmunks and birds to entertain us. The crested jays and magpies scolded us. One day a porcupine came to investigate us. Kathleen and Patsy cuddled up close to me on either side while the porcupine smelled us all over and then rattled on his way to climb a nearby tree and start tearing off bark to eat. Water ouzels had a nest nearby. It was almost unbelievable to see them fly under the water and walk along the floor of the stream gathering feed for their young, then fly out, wet feathers and all, just as if they weren't wet at all. Trout came out from behind the big boulders and fed on the insects that lit on the surface of the stream.

Fall term came and Kathleen entered the first grade. The doctor had given us a very satisfactory report. Grammar school, high school and college seemed to follow in such rapid succession that Juanita and I wondered where the time has flown.

Yesterday we had Sunday dinner with Kathleen and Paul, our son-in-law, and our three darling grandchildren, Ann, eight, Tommy, five, and Billy, three. I am sure that no one could be happier than our family, but how Kathleen gets everything done that she has to do with her home and family, and still finds time for clubs and entertaining we do not know. We do know that we owe a great debt of gratitude to Patsy.

But, although her help in curing Kathleen was Patsy's greatest achievement, the blessing that this puppy brought to our household does not end here.

There used to be a saying among dog men: "After you have spoiled three dogs you will have learned enough to train one." There is a good deal of truth in this, although no one needs to make as many mistakes as most of us do. Today anyone can find enough good advice in books and in classes to avoid spoiling more than one dog at most. Our first mistake with Patsy was that we bought a four-month-old puppy instead of one that was only seven or eight weeks of age as we should have done. Later we explain why it is so grave a mistake.

Even though I had been attracted to them since before I could remember, I had never understood the relationship of a dog to his master. This is the sad thing so many of us experience unnecessarily. We expect our children to be able to learn patiently and carefully to do the things we wish them to do from the time we think they should be able to say a few words or walk. Somehow, most of us do not realize that a dog needs an education just as much as a child, that he needs to learn what our different words mean, what a gesture means, and what we mean by different whistles. He does not understand our language, nor does our baby for that matter. We have to show what we mean. With understanding and patience, a dog can be taught many things. He can also learn to understand many words for their exact meaning.

I must confess that Patsy was almost a complete loss so far as being a well-trained dog goes. Her great value was in what she did to help Kathleen regain her health and what she did for us in giving birth to The Master Blue Print, a blue roan who could have been one of America's great field trial cocker spaniels, had I known the things which I have learned in the last fourteen years. His call name was Cal.

I had studied pedigrees and knew how to pick out important individuals in the pedigrees, but I had no idea how to use a pedigree to tell me how to produce an important animal.

One day Juanita brought home a book written by Mr. H. S. Lloyd, of the "Of Ware Kennels" in England, entitled the *English Cocker Spaniel*. I read this with interest and, knowing that Patsy had some English cocker ancestors (the cocker at that time had not been divided into American and English breeds, and both were used by many breeders without any discrimination), I got out Patsy's pedigree and was pleasantly surprised to find that a number of the dogs in her pedigree were listed and illustrated in this book as examples of the best England had produced.

We both admired the blue roan color and so we consulted the

Hunts as to whom we could breed Patsy to in order to get blue roan puppies. They suggested that we breed her to her father, Burhan's Little Boy Blue, who was blue roan and whose mother had come from Mr. Lloyd's stock. I had no idea at that time that this is just what a geneticist would have told me, not only to get blue roans, but to get the good qualities I admired in Burhan's Little Boy Blue, nor had I the slightest notion that some day I would be a party to a breeding program which produced hundreds of German shepherds from father to daughter, thus producing excellent results which did not surprise geneticists. Why this is true, and the amazing results we have gotten at Guide Dogs for the Blind, Inc., is also another chapter.

With our appetite for knowledge about dogs whetted by Mr. Lloyd's book, we started to buy dog magazines and outdoor magazines. Another Lloyd, also English, Mr. Freeman Lloyd, was at that time writing for *Field and Stream*. He was a skillful story teller and a great booster for the spaniel breeds as the ideal hunters for Americans. He also told about spaniel field trials at Fisher's Island, New York. I had not had an opportunity to hunt for some time, but I decided that Cal should be a hunter.

One evening there was a notice in one of the San Francisco newspapers that there would be a meeting that evening, when spaniel owners could see a film of spaniels hunting and be told how to train a spaniel. Juanita, Helenjoy, Kathleen and I were in the front seats. The film showed Mr. A. M. "Monty" Lewis working two of his famous American cocker spaniels, Latch Up George and Latch Up Porge, on all kinds of game birds.

The group present had a long discussion about how we could work together to train our dogs. It lasted so long that Juanita and the girls left the smoke-filled room for fresher air in our car. When I finally came out of the meeting, Juanita wanted to know what had happened. I said, "A field trial training club was organized."

She said, "I hope you did not join it."

I said, "Yes, I did, and was elected president."

She asked, "How much did it cost you?"

I answered, "Fifteen dollars."

"Fifteen dollars," Juanita repeated incredulously. "Oh, how

many things I could buy for the girls with fifteen dollars."

That was the beginning of the only spaniel field trial club west of Chicago which had been formed up to that time, and which is still in existence.

The old breaking methods, instead of educational ones, were in general practice, and none of us knew any better until Mr. Evan George joined our club and began to preach teaching instead of breaking. We learned a lot from him. He had had experience in New England.

Although Juanita was shocked at the initial investment, she has always been a good sport. When my doctors found that my work with dogs was having a great beneficial effect on my health she turned to with a will. Before long we were in dogs up to our ears as a hobby. We have never been in dogs as a profession or a business, but we have bred many fine dogs. One of Cal's daughters gave birth to three dogs to win their titles: Field Trial Champion Roanfeather Argonaut, Ch. Waite's Peter Pan, and Roanfeather Peter U.D. And, as a bonus, she gave us Skookie.

Most of us have had experiences which leave a lasting impression. These are often isolated, and, unless they are bolstered by the same or similar experiences repeated in a similar pattern, they cannot be accepted as much more than a coincidence. Juanita and I had such an experience with Skookie. The importance of this experience did not become entirely clear to us until several years later, when Dr. Scott discovered the "critical periods in the life of a puppy" at the Roscoe B. Jackson Memorial Laboratory in Bar Harbor, Maine. I believe that you will better understand the critical periods which are explained in other chapters if I tell you about Skookie.

From Skookie we had our first lesson in starting to train a puppy very young, but it was a dozen years later that we learned why this was important. Meanwhile we had raised, trained, and shown a great many dogs, and I had screened several thousand dogs for the armed forces and taught more than a thousand people how to train dogs.

I have said that one of Cal's daughters gave us a bonus of Skookie.

When he was born, a lonely one-pup litter, we named him

35

"Surplus." He was the last thing we wanted and we thought that he was the last thing we needed. He proved us wrong, and taught us a wonderful lesson which becomes more and more important through the years as we have learned to understand the truth and why it is the truth.

His mother, "Roanfeather Bonbon," had twelve points toward her show championship and had been winning points consistently when she came home to rest up while she was in season.

His father was Mrs. Pfaffenberger's "Champion Peirson's Cream Puff."

The breeding was not planned by us.

The ringing of the telephone, a careless moment on my part while I answered it, and the mother's show career was postponed. Fifty-nine days later we had "Surplus." That was all.

Later when we saw what a delightful little fellow he was we repented and registered him with the American Kennel Club as "Roanfeather Sir Plus," a name that turned out to be especially fitting.

Because Skookie was the only puppy we had at the time, he got a lot of handling. Before he could see me or hear me I had fallen in love with him, and was picking him up whenever I was near his nest, petting him and calling him nice little baby names. When at last his eyes focused and his ears opened, he found himself getting special attention and showed a delight in my daily visits with him. When he was four weeks old I started to give him some simple lessons. I made a very small wooden dummy for him and covered it with quail wings. He took to this at once and was making nice deliveries to hand by six weeks of age with real enthusiasm.

By the time Skookie was twelve weeks of age he was doing excellent dummy retrieving, with the larger dummies I used for the grown dogs, from tall thick grass. Then I started to teach him to quarter the ground by running with him in the field to about thirty yards to one side of a center line and then to the other side, always turning back in such a way as to advance about fifteen feet down the field by the time we returned to the starting side. This I did to teach him a good working pattern by which he could hunt a field thoroughly, so as not to miss any

36

game, but at the same time going ahead about as fast as a good hunter will walk in the field. Each time we turned I would blow two quick, sharp blasts on my whistle. This was to teach him that when the whistle blew he was to turn.

As soon as he had learned to turn on the whistle I stopped running with him as he quartered, but instead I walked down the center line and whistled when he reached the limit of his cast. To make it more interesting for him and more practical, I next had Skookie sit where he could see me take a feathered dummy out in the field about fifty yards. Then I would cast him, first to one side and then to the other in his regular quartering pattern, until he came within scenting distance of the dummy. At that time I would encourage him to charge in. As soon as he had picked up the dummy I would blow the "come" whistle, but instead of standing and waiting for him to complete the retrieve I would turn and run toward our car, blowing the "come" signal, which is a trill. This taught him to make his retrieve as fast as he could run. The hurrying caused him to learn to get a good hold on the dummy so he would not drop it. Part way to the car I would stop and wait for him, and when he sat in front of me with the dummy in his mouth I would praise him and then ask him to give. Thus, I taught him to make a fast, stylish retrieve and to deliver to hand gently.

One day when the other club members and I were training older dogs for a field trial to be held at Santa Cruz a month later, there were a few pigeons left over from training the older dogs and I asked one of our club members to plant three for Skookie. He had never flushed a bird from cover.

I started him on the course just as if he were going to hunt for the dummies he had been accustomed to retrieving for me. He quartered nicely and all of a sudden his head went high and he started working in on the first planted pigeon. When he flushed it I said, "Skookie hup!" and he sat and held steady while the bird was shot and until I gave him the command to fetch. Upon command, he was off at full steam; he had marked the bird fall well; he picked up the pigeon smartly and brought it directly back to me where he sat and held it for me to take. He worked out the other two birds faultlessly. It was then that I decided to enter him in the Santa Cruz Spaniel Field Trial. His bird work had been superb and his deliveries a delight to behold.

There were to be four stakes for cocker spaniels at Santa Cruz. Three of them were listed as "minor stakes," puppy, amateur trained and handled, and limit. I was so enthused about the pup that I entered him in all three of these. When I arrived at the trial site, I looked at the entries in the catalog and was alarmed to find nearly all of the open-all-age stake dogs (championship) were also entered in the amateur trained and handled class. I could see that this was going to be a severe test for a puppy.

I was not prepared for two things that were to happen. When the dogs were called up for the amateur trained and handled stake the bird planters put down pheasants instead of pigeons. Skookie had never seen a pheasant before. There was nothing to do but to run him on pheasants and I did it with a lot of trepidation. I need not have been jittery. My dog had full confidence in me. He had always done anything I asked him to do. He did it now. He flushed his pheasants, held steady to flush and shot and made long, spectacular retrieves.

It was like having a wonderful dream. I could scarcely believe what was happening was really happening. In the past I had trained my dogs by the generally accepted methods and at the time in life when most people train their dogs, around six or eight months at the youngest. Dogs trained by those methods and at that time in their lives had always kept me on edge at every trial, wondering if I could control my dogs. If something unexpected should happen, which was almost sure to occur, would they respond to my commands or would they "get away from me"? Now, here before me, I had a dog with a natural instinct to hunt, but who had been trained in a positive manner from the time he had been capable of learning, and I had not the slightest worry about what he would do. I knew he would do what I asked him to do.

Or did I? If what I heard over the loudspeaker was correct we still had a test which might well be our downfall.

What I had heard was correct. "All amateur trained and handled dogs will be taken to the lake on the south side of the field trial site for the water test."

For some reason or another I had never had Skookie in the water, and I realized for the first time that this was one part of his lessons which I had neglected. It is always good to start a spaniel in water young, and I do not know now how I had overlooked this with Skookie, but the truth was he had never retrieved from water. I had never asked him to.

Skookie and I wandered over to the lake, which was actually an inlet from the Pacific Ocean. I stood there looking across the water and saw the puppy's chance of winning a place in this stake go glimmering.

"That's some pup you have got there." The voice was that of Roy Gonia, a great professional handler.

"He sure is," chimed in Ed Williams, official gun. They had come up quietly so that I had not known they were there.

"He IS a wonderful pup," I said. "But he has never been in water."

At that moment a pigeon which had escaped from one of the early land series flew overhead.

"Shoot it, Ed," said Roy.

Ed dropped it nicely on the land, just beyond the inlet.

"Fetch, Skookie," I said.

Skookie leaped out into the deep water, swam across the inlet, picked up the bird and delivered it nicely to my hand after a return swim.

A few minutes later the judges came up and Skookie was called up first for the water test. Ed Williams was selected to shoot. He dropped the new bird close to where he had dropped the first one.

Skookie made a faultless retrieve.

Half an hour later when the trophies were handed out, Skookie was awarded first prize in both puppy and limit stakes and third in amateur trained and handled.

If it had not been for a chain of circumstances that might never happen again in a life time, an accidental breeding, a one-pup litter, time to handle and train the little fellow, maybe a little shame at having harshly called him "Surplus," and the accidental choice of time in his puppy life and proper methods of training him, Skookie would, probably, have been sold to someone as an ordinary cocker spaniel pet. I would have never realized what a great little fellow he was, or that starting a puppy in positive training at a very early age is the best way to mold him into the kind of dog that you want him to be.

Last year I let sorrel get in my lily bed. All winter I shoveled yards of earth and screened it to get this pest and the roots out of the soil.

To allow a puppy to grow up his own way, learn what he wants to learn, sow his wild oats before the owner starts to train him to do things the way he wants them done, can result in just as back-breaking a job as I had extricating the weeds from my lily bulbs. What is worse, having frittered away this valuable time when he should have been started in training not only allows the puppy to pick up undesirable habits which will be hard, if not impossible, to correct, but the time lost is the most valuable in a puppy's life for his socialization. It will never come again. To waste it is like letting gold flow through your fingers down into the ocean. It is forever lost.

Almost every chapter in this book will deal in some way with different things I learned from Patsy, Cal and Skookie. The trouble was that I had no way of properly evaluating what I learned and very often I misinterpreted the meanings. This is bound to be true, with too small an opportunity to gather enough data to be worth analyzing, and with those of us who are not well enough informed in the technics of analysis of statistical data to get at the true meaning. In the last fifteen years I have learned why Skookie was so great. I will show you, too, in the chapters that follow.

CHAPTER III

How Our Dogs Served the Nation's People

The little club which had been formed that night at the Whitcomb Hotel started out with less than a dozen members, owners of cocker spaniels and springer spaniels. It was called the Spaniel Training Club. Its purpose was for the members to get together with their dogs, pool their knowledge, and get help whenever they could to train their spaniels for hunting and maybe field trials.

There were to be monthly meetings in the field where the dogs would be trained. Meanwhile, each member would teach his dog what he had learned at the previous meeting. We could drive to a good training area in less than a half hour. Soon, spaniel owners from Monterey to Turlock and Sacramento were coming to these monthly meets and you could count on at least twenty spaniel owners with their dogs being present at each monthly meeting.

The interest was so great there was considerable demand for Spaniel Field Trials. Eventually our training club applied for permission to put on, first, a sanctioned, and then a licensed, trial. Both proved very popular. They became so popular with the general public that the state highway patrol had to take charge of the traffic.

There were many developments from these trials which shaped for Juanita and me the courses that our dog interests were to

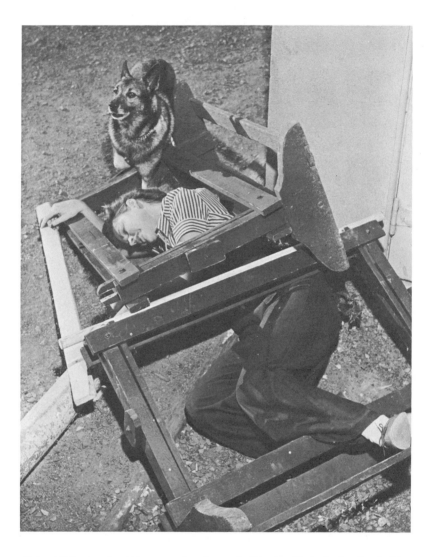

Colonel Richardson taught his rescue dogs to search off lead and to bark when they had located a victim. We found that working dogs, terriers and Norwegian elkhounds worked well this way. Most other hounds and almost all sporting dogs refused to bark while working. Pictured here is "Storm King," a Norwegian elkhound who has found his victim, Mrs. Robert Kemph.

take. Over a period of a few years our dog activities were to lead us indirectly to our interest in Guide Dogs for the Blind, Inc., and our association with the testing, breeding, and rearing of these most interesting dogs. Our search for the nearly perfect puppy for a Guide Dog would never have started had it not been for the trials and the chain of events which followed.

Meanwhile we started collecting dog books. There is a surprisingly large number of excellent books about dogs. Some are real collector's items. Some of the best are among the oldest. There have also been some excellent ones written in the last twenty-five years. One needs the best from the past to go with the best from the present to make a well-rounded dog library.

At the start, our club was very inexperienced in field trial matters. The officers of governing bodies to whom we were responsible for the manner in which the trials were conducted, and from whom we had to obtain permission to put on licensed trials, were all in New York. They were: Mr. Henry D. Bixby, Executive Vice-President, American Kennel Club; Mr. Harry I. Caesar, Secretary, English Springer Spaniel Field Trial Association; and Mr. A. M. "Monty" Lewis, Secretary, American Spaniel Club.

With the tremendous interest that had developed in Spaniel Field Trials in California, new clubs having sprung up and new dog owners constantly joining the ranks, there was bound to come a time when there would not be a meeting of all the minds. So when an exhibitor wrote a critical letter of one of our trials, in 1940, our club found itself without a license to continue trials. It was not that we were accused of wrongdoing; it was just that it was impossible to clearly explain what had happened to so many people so far away.

We had grown so fast, but there was something which we had not understood: we were so different. Spaniel Trials had been The Sport of the English Gentlemen. When these trials were imported to the United States many of the field trial dogs, their trainers, and even stewards and judges were brought to Fisher's Island to put on the first trial.

Out here in California, a group of people unknown even in their own state had organized clubs, trained dogs, run trials. It

43

just was not logical that we could be doing anything like what the Field Trial had been intended to be. It is rather surprising that we had been allowed to start at all with so little preparation. Naturally a severe protest must have confirmed fears which may have existed in the minds of these three wonderful gentlemen from the first. They had been good sports, but they loved their dogs and the Spaniel Field Trials dearly and they would not countenance anything that would do Spaniel Trials discredit. No sports events ever had finer guardians of their well-being. What had happened seemed like such a little thing to the club, but it must have been reported very effectively, because we were denied trial privileges.

That "the darkest hour is just before the dawn" has so often proved to be true in my life. So often, when I felt that the bottom had dropped out completely, this was just the turning point to better things which I could not see around the corner. I have said that Juanita had always been a good sport about our dogs. You will see what I mean. When she saw that we were up against a stone wall she said, "We will go back and talk to these men. You write and get an appointment to see them. When summer vacation comes we will drive back."

I said, "We do not have the money."

She said, "Our credit is good. We will borrow the money."

We had decided that since we were going East we should make the most of it, take the girls on a trip through as many states and to as many important places as possible. We decided also to see some of the famous spaniels in the states east of the Mississippi. Juanita was born in Maine so we had a large trip planned. The trip took in the Grand Canyon, the Painted Desert, the Carlsbad Caverns, Washington, D.C., Mount Vernon, Boston and the land of the pilgrims, New York, Maine, Niagara Falls, the Colorado Rockies, and Salt Lake, to name but a few or the places, and many of the great kennels such as Idahurst, Belfield, My Own, and Lauren T. Miller's. That was in the summer of 1941, the trip we had always planned for our girls and ourselves. A few months later it would have been impossible.

Once we were settled, I telephoned to Mr. Lewis and he invited Juanita and me down to spend Sunday at his home in

Stamford, Connecticut. We had a lovely day and formed a friendship which lasted until Mr. Lewis' death last year. He was one of the best friends I ever made among all the wonderful dog people I have known. He worked George and Porgie for me. They were wonderfully trained and magnificent workers. We had a nice, leisurely day in which I learned a great deal about field trials. On Tuesday I had an appointment to meet Mr. Caesar at his office in New York. Helenjoy and Kathleen went with me, and while I called on Mr. Caesar they visited National Camp Fire Girls Headquarters and were conducted on a tour.

Mr. Caesar was most cordial and kept me talking all morning. He wanted to know about us, our club, rather than tell me about the Eastern Spaniel Field Trials. He wanted to know how we started, how we conducted our trials, how we financed them, who planted the birds, who were the official guns, and who were the club members. At last it began to dawn on me that our club, as field trial clubs went, was sort of a freak. At least it was very different from clubs where members had little worry about finances, professional game-bird breeder planters, and the choice of the best sites. Most of the dog owners had their spaniels trained by professionals, although many of the owners ran the dogs in the trials. Finally, Mr. Caesar said, "There is a club something like yours up at Albany, but I believe that yours is different from any we know anything about. I'd like to make an appointment for you with Mr. Bixby. Can you go to see him this afternoon?"

After he had made the appointment Mr. Caesar said, "You tell Mr. Bixby just what you have told me."

After I had spent a couple of hours telling about our club, Mr. Bixby told me that I could go home assured that we could hold our 1941 field trial. At that trial I caught a bad cold and so missed the trial at Stockton the next weekend. After the trial at Stockton, Roy and Juanda Gonia came directly to our house to spend the night. They hadn't had the radio on and since they had started very early they had not heard that Japan had struck at Pearl Harbor.

Earlier, at one of our field trial practice meets during the early fall of 1941, the weather had been so hot that we had worked early, had lunch, and then sat around talking. Evan George suggested that sooner or later we would be drawn into the war, and that the dog people should be readying their dogs for rescue work so that lives could be saved from fallen debris when the bombs started to fall. The chance seemed remote, but we decided to see if our dogs would alert us to a person hidden in the field. Some of them did very well, and we decided to meet in San Francisco once a week to train them for this work. At first Mr. George had charge of the class. Later, when he became ill and had to give it up, I took it over.

We were meeting regularly when the bombs fell on Pearl Harbor. Shortly after this the American Legion County Council and the American Red Cross Chapter, who jointly had charge of civilian defense in San Francisco, heard about our group and asked us to join them officially. This we did, but as things got going the school department set up classes for many things to aid in the war effort. My evening school principal, Dr. Charles J. Lamp, became interested in the dog classes and arranged with state and city school officials to incorporate them into the war effort classes. I was given a credential in teaching Dogs for Rescue and Defense, and we announced that dog owners who wished to help by training and handling their dogs in Rescue and Defense work might enroll.

The football field between the school and the San Francisco Opera House proved to be a suitable place for the training of Dogs for Rescue and Defense. The field was only lighted by the street lights on the four sides and the bleachers were excellent for concealing the pseudo-victims.

The purpose of a rescue dog, in an area where there has been bombing or an earthquake which has buried people in debris, is to locate where the persons are buried so that rescuers can dig them out before they suffocate or die from other injuries. At first we thought the victims would have to be covered to develop the proper understanding in the dog's mind that he was searching for a buried person. We found that all we needed to do was have the victim lie down and remain lying perfectly still. The victim would go to his place of hiding by some other route than the dog would take, and while the dog was not in a position to see him going. This was to prevent the dog from tracking or trying to find a person by remembering where he last saw someone go out of sight. Later, when persons were hidden under all kinds of old lumber or any kind of materials, the dogs located them perfectly. When a victim was located by a trained dog the handler would rush up, help the victim to his feet, and then both the victim and the handler would praise the dog profusely. This done, they would return to the place from which the dog had been sent to search.

Lieutenant Colonel Edwin Hauteville Richardson had charge of the training of rescue dogs in England and his dogs were doing a remarkable rescue job in the bombed-out areas. Although it seemed like a very inopportune time to bother so busy a man, I wrote to Colonel Richardson. He and his wife were most cooperative and supplied me with their method of training. I was also able to get two books from Colonel Richardson which he had written on the subject.

Colonel Richardson had used mostly Airedales and collies. The method he used was first to train a dog to look for a prone or supine figure. Once the victim was found, the dog was trained to sit down beside the person and bark. As soon as the dog learned this he was allowed to search free, off leash. The dog had to remain and continue to bark until aid came and the victim was freed. Airedales and collies are two breeds which are especially inclined to bark. This method worked very well for Colonel Richardson.

My group of rescue personnel was made up entirely of volunteer dog owners and their dogs. I had no choice as to breeds or even to the age or previous training the dog had had. Everyone who offered his or her service was accepted and an attempt made to train the trainer and the dog. The thing that developed now was that some of the dogs would learn to bark when they found a victim and some would not. Soon we realized that all spaniels, setters, pointers and some hounds were the dogs who refused to bark when they found their hidden persons. Collies, shepherds, elkhounds, and most working breeds would bark. This boiled down to the fact that the breeds who did not bark were the same breeds who had been selected for not barking while working, because they would disturb the game. These are character traits which have been bred into these breeds so strongly by selective breeding that even when they were asked to bark they would not do so. The same dogs would bark at home if someone came to the door, but not at work in the field.

At first we tried to teach these dogs to bark on command. Most of them would do this, but would get completely lost from their owner while searching for a victim, because they did not give tongue at work. So we decided to work these dogs on a long line and let them lead us to our victims. This worked so well that we taught all breeds to work this way.

Once we had arrived at a desirable method of working our Rescue Dogs, we would put a tracking harness on the dog, attach a long line just before we wanted him to search, and remove the harness as soon as he had found his victim. Thus, the harness and what the dog was to do were firmly established in the dog's mind. Although he had no scented trail to follow, as soon as the harness was in place, the line attached, and the direction he was to go indicated by a hand signal, he would race off in search of his victim, taking his owner with him at the end of the line. When he picked up the scent of a person sitting or lying down, he would dash to that person's side and wait for his handler to come to render aid. It was amazing how soon most dogs learned to pick up the scent of a person lying down or sitting, in contrast to one standing up. I do not know the explanation for this ability to detect this difference, but it surely does happen, even when other persons are standing in rather close proximity to the person lying down.

Here are two of the humorous incidents that happened as our dogs advanced in their training. The last one indicates how well this distinction was established.

One night, as the class filed out of the gate at the stadium, I was saying good night to each when I saw a hobo climb the low wall along Van Ness Avenue. He had a bundle on his back and he headed for the stands on the opposite side of the field from where I stood. There he unrolled his blankets and proceeded to make a bed on one of the seats. Just as he was well to bed, Russel Grant, who had an excellent working Australian blue sheep dog,

Buddie, came by. Buddie was one of the dogs who had learned to work on his own and to sit down by the victim and bark in the English Rescue Dog style. On impulse, I stopped Mr. Grant and said, "There is a man lying over in those bleachers. Stay here, but send Buddie to see if he can find him."

On command, Buddie was off on his own to search for a victim. When he reached the far side of the field, he methodically searched the stands from top to bottom until he picked up the scent and then, noiselessly, he dashed to the side of the tramp, sat down and let out a blood-curdling howl. For once Buddie's victim did not wait to be rescued, but sprang to his feet and, with blankets trailing behind him like some angel from the underworld in flight, hurdled the north wall of the stadium and disappeared in the direction of the Opera House.

The other incident happened to my dog, Skookie, whom I had trained for this work. As soon as our dogs were working satisfactorily each one of us in the class was assigned to work with a Red Cross Rescue Unit. The first night that I reported with Skookie I explained to the Captain what Skookie and I were supposed to do.

"O.K., let's see you work," the captain told me. Saying this he stepped aside and called an assistant to him and directed him where to hide in the Junior High School building they were using for their training. The building was entirely dark and neither Skookie nor I had any way of knowing where the victim had gone to hide. When the captain thought that his man had had plenty of time to hide he led us to an entrance, which I had specified should be other than the one where the victim entered. This was to make sure that Skookie would not be tracking rather than rescue searching. There were fifteen or twenty adults in this captain's team, and even more children watching.

"Is it O.K. if these other people go along? They would like to see how you work," the captain explained.

"Certainly. Let them all come. It will be O.K. just as long as none of them sits or lies down," I told him.

"Now all of you stay behind Mr. Pfaffenberger and his dog," the captain warned.

"That isn't necessary," I interrupted. "Let them walk anywhere they like. Skookie is only looking for a prostrate body."

So the crowd swirled around us, almost as badly as it might in real panic. Skookie paid not the least attention to those walking, nor even to some who stood lined up against the wall to let us pass. We had done all of the first floor without the slightest indication from Skookie that there was a victim in the building which occupied half a block and was built in an "L." We climbed to the second floor. Skookie raced along down the center of the corridor, around the corner, and, about half way down the long leg of the building, he turned abruptly and stopped in front of the door to a classroom. I opened the door and followed him around two sides of the room to the teacher's desk in the far corner. I could hear the captain telling some of his squad that we had made a mistake. He said the victim was not even on this floor.

"Please turn on the light," I requested.

From under the teacher's desk I dragged two red-faced boys, their pockets bulging with loot.

Although I praised Skookie, this was one time the victims did not praise their rescuer.

So we raced on down that floor to the stairs at the end, up the stairs to the third floor, and down the hall to about the same distance as the room we had entered on the second floor. The victim had opened all the classroom doors, thinking that Skookie could not smell him if the door was closed, and so as not to indicate which room he was in. Here we found the victim who had been sent to hide.

"I thought you were going to fail to find me when I heard you downstairs, and was just about ready to come back when I heard you come up to this floor. What happened down there?" he wanted to know.

The captain was very apologetic as he explained that we had found two other victims, whom he still had in tow.

Before the end of the war we had developed twenty reliable man-dog rescue teams, owners with their dogs all working with Red Cross Rescue teams in San Francisco.

Meanwhile, back around New York, dog owners had been offering their services with their dogs. Many trained their own

50

dogs and offered them to the armed services for the duration. The movement caught on and Dogs for Defense was organized. Soon all over the country dog people were offering their services with their dogs, or their trained dogs for service. Our organization was drafted into the Dogs for Defense setup. Mr. Harry I. Caesar was chosen as National President of Dogs for Defense, and Mr. A. M. "Monty" Lewis as National Treasurer. With such a responsible group offering its help the Army, Coast Guard and Marine Corps all decided to try dogs for limited service. The first dogs were so helpful that soon large War Dog Reception and Training Centers were set up to train military men and dogs for all types of service: guard duty, scouting, messenger, and eventually mine detection.

It was decided that one of the largest centers would be located at San Carlos, on the San Francisco Peninsula. Mrs. Milton Erlanger, one of the National Officers of Dogs for Defense, came to San Francisco and asked me if I would be willing to be the regional director for Northern California. I said that I could not afford to give up my teaching job. I had to make a living. She said that she would like to talk with the superintendent of schools, if I had no objection, and tell him that Mr. Caesar and Mr. Lewis felt that I was needed for the job. To my surprise I was called to the superintendent's office a few days later and informed that the board of education had voted to loan me to Dogs for Defense for the duration. The board of education provided me with a well-equipped office for Dogs for Defense, and a vacant school yard and storage room. These were used for assembling dogs and testing them for acceptability and for storing empty dog crates.

During the next three years I screened several thousand dogs who were offered by their owners to help win the war. More than 1,800 of these dogs were accepted by the armed forces. Also, a number were supplied to Seeing Eye, Morristown, New Jersey.

It was about this time that I began to realize how closely knit was our Dogs for Defense and Rescue training class. As soon as the papers announced that my office was open, mail started to pour in offering dogs for the service. I was swamped, and men-

51

tioned it at class one night. The next day when I came to my office I found my mail all opened and sorted on my desk. There was a card file system set up. Volunteers had come from my rescue class. Virginia Williams had organized a filing system for me. Her mother, Mrs. Lenore Williams, had taken the telephone over and took the messages which poured in. As soon as I had the office organized to a point where I could use more help, volunteers came as fast I could use them: Mrs. James Fry, Mrs. Ray Dougherty, Mrs. James F. Duncan, Mrs. E. A. Leach, and Mrs. Ron Tessier. Most Saturdays we had to work also, and Miss Marjorie Grinnel recruited a staff for the weekends. There were many more, but these helped throughout the entire time that my office was in operation, which included the demobilization of the dogs as well as the procurement.

Of all the dogs who came home, we had only one bad report. That was caused by someone giving the dog a command to attack to show what his dog could do. But we had daily classes at the end of the war to instruct each dog owner on what to do and what not to do to avoid just this. It worked.

Captain J. Stanley Head trained at the San Carlos Center. He is well known now as a leading field trial professional. Captain Head commanded war dog units in all the major campaigns from Guadalcanal to Japan, and was many times decorated. Stan told me that his scout dogs were always eager to serve. He and his men learned to accept their dogs' judgment and to accept what their dogs' actions told them in preference to their own judgment. A dog can hear much higher and lower sounds than a person can. His sense of smell has never been satisfactorily evaluated, but it is so superior that we do not yet understand its workings. A dog's eyes are different from ours. One very valuable quality is his ability to practically photograph motion. Where we might be aware that something moved, a dog will know just where it moved.

In May, 1944, five American soldiers and their commanding officer returned from jungle campaigns in New Guinea and New Britain credited officially with having disposed of more than two hundred enemy soldiers. They returned to the United States without having received a scratch from an enemy knife or bullet.

There were no casualties. All the enemy had been taken completely by surprise.

This was the record of the first Army K-9 Corps men to return from the war zone. I was given official permission to interview these men as soon as they arrived and to write their story. In the months that followed, many similar stories of the exploits of our K-9 Corps men and their dogs on our front lines and on many fronts came to me officially, as Regional Director of Dogs for Defense. It was here that I learned for the first time the importance of dogs who can take responsibility, and the fact that a great many dogs cannot take responsibility. It was many years later that we discovered why some dogs cannot take responsibility. That is told in another chapter.

How very valuable are the dogs who can take responsibility is illustrated by the following information. For forty-eight out of fifty-three days in New Guinea alone, these men and their six scout dogs and two messenger dogs spearheaded the reconnaisance patrols of the Australian jungle fighters in the Markham Valley and the Ramu Valley. Never did the enemy surprise them or ambush them, and neither they nor their reconnaissance suffered a single casualty while disposing of the enemy according to plan.

Second Lieutenant Robert Johnson, Malden, Massachusetts, commanding officer; Sergeant Guy Sheldon, Montpelier, New Hampshire; Sergeant William Jorgensen, Pleasant Grove, Utah; Sergeant Arthur N. Tyler, Livingston Manor, New York; Sergeant Herman Boude, Chillicothe, Missouri; and Sergeant Menzo S. Brown, Middletown, New York, were the hollow-eyed, jungle-skilled heroes who made up the returning band. Each gave full credit to his dog for the phenomenal success he had had in carrying out his most dangerous assignment. These men with their dogs had opened up areas which would have been impassable without their dogs. No troops had gotten through the ambuscades of the Japanese who had taken over one side of the island and held it for months until the six American K-9 Corps men with six scout dogs and two messenger dogs cleared a path which led the Australian troops across and helped clean out the entire pocket of enemy.

These were very quiet-spoken men. They had to be asked questions. When they talked they were often near the emotional breaking point. Months of near silence; months of scouting, stalking, capturing, destroying in a jungle; then, suddenly, to find that they were back where life was almost normal, even in war, was just about all human nature could bear. But their loyalty to their dogs and their great admiration for these superb animals was a revelation of how close a man-dog team can grow to one another. Quiet approach had been the key to their success. Now they were much like nuns from a cloister who find themselves suddenly back in the hurly-burly noises and racing motions of the modern world.

"It was pretty grim," they admitted. "We and our dogs shared the same rations, drank from the same water, slept together in our foxholes. We faced a common enemy. We destroyed a common foe. Dogs and men, Men and dogs, our military career was one. The way we felt about our dogs out there is that our dogs are just as much persons to us as we are to each other."

Eight months previously, these men had gone into a trackless jungle with eight dogs to determine the true value and usefulness of dogs under combat conditions where the Japanese had long impeded the progress of the Australian jungle fighting soldiers and the American Marines. They went in where telephone wires could not be strung; where radar and walkie talkie were not practical on account of the plant life and weather. Extreme dampness greatly hampered the operation of such equipment.

The importance of the service of the dogs can best be calculated by the fact that a point-man without a dog on such a tour would have had less than a fifty per cent chance of survival, while none of these dogs or the men they led suffered a single casualty.

To me this is one of the supreme examples of how dogs will take the responsibility of man's safety, for the scouts depended upon their dogs not only to avoid ambushes and traps, but to lead them to the enemy. There were many cases where the enemy and scouts passed each other, or the scouts penetrated through the enemy lines to reconnoiter. Their dogs would lead them by a safe route both ways without alerting the enemy.

One of the most unusual and almost unbelievable examples of a dog taking responsibility came when these six men and eight dogs were engaged in landing at Cape Gloucester, New Britain.

Sergeant Sheldon and Sergeant Brown were detailed to provide communications between the front line and the main body of troops. Their messenger dog, a German shepherd named Sandy, and Sergeant Brown went ashore with the first wave and stayed constantly in the forefront of the attack, with the regimental scouts pushing their way over a narrow strip of beach. Here the enemy 75 mm artillery and machine guns in pillboxes prevented the main body of troops from landing.

The second day, Brown with the advance was cut off completely from the main body. Radio and other communications were blanked out by a torrential downpour. This battle took place on December 28, 1943. At 1 p.m. Sergeant Brown with the assault company located the positions of the pillboxes. A map was drawn showing their exact positions. This was placed with a note in Sandy's collar and she was dispatched with the message for the battalion commanding officer.

Sandy had been taught to work only with Sergeant Brown and Sergeant Sheldon. The only information Brown had before the communications were cut off was that Sergeant Sheldon had been landed on an isolated point somewhere east of where Brown and the assault troops were. Neither Brown nor Sandy had seen where Sheldon had landed, and had not been in communication with him for more than twenty-four hours. The command post for which Sergeant Sheldon directed communications had been moved several times during the day which had elapsed. At the time that Sandy was sent with the message, the post was in a foxhole surrounded by a barbed wire entanglement, completely obscured from the human eye.

To reach Sheldon, Sandy had to locate her human partner in some place east of where she started. She had to carry her message through heavy cannon and machine gun fire, fight her way through almost impenetrable kuni grass; cross several creeks; swim a river; slip across a road on an open beach where the enemy was bringing up supplies—and then find her man.

Sergeant Sheldon in his foxhole was trying desperately to

reach Brown by radio telephone when he was startled to see Sandy come sailing over the barbed wire into his arms. Sheldon had communication with the landing force still on board and with the destroyer along side. He took the message from Sandy's collar, transmitted it to the ships, and was told to tell Brown at what time the barrage would wipe out the pillboxes and artillery. The reply was placed in Sandy's collar. She was let out of the enclosure and at once made a prompt return to Brown, having safely run messages twice under the enemy's nose without a scratch except from the jungle. The Japanese position was destroyed and the allied troops landed.

"It is believed that no human runner could have possibly gotten through the withering fire that our enemy was laying down," the official report on this action reads.

On many fronts, under many different circumstances, the War Dogs of the United States armed forces did many services, scouting, running messages, guarding supplies and locating land mines so they could be safely removed to allow our troops to pass. Many of these duties were at night, when the acute senses of smell and hearing made the service of the dog so very valuable. These six men and eight dogs did all their work by daylight, often within a short distance of the enemy and still *there were no casualties*.

CHAPTER IV

Dog's Place In Human Progress Understood

In the fever pitch of war activity following Pearl Harbor all loyal citizens searched their hearts, their purses, and their attics for things they could contribute which would help most in defeating the enemies. There was nowhere, perhaps, where the sincerity of this patriotic urge was so clearly exemplified as by so many dog owners giving their personal canine companions to Dogs for Defense to be loaned to the various United States armed services for the duration of the war. To many of those who gave their dogs the sacrifice was only exceeded by giving up a member of their family to go to war. Many families gave both their children and their dogs. Had these dog owners banded together deliberately to help our dogs find their place in civilization, they could never have found a better time or a better opportunity to do just that.

As terrible as wars are they have always accelerated progress in certain directions. Perhaps the word "advancement" in these directions is more exact than progress. Since World War II, these have been most noticeable in medicine, atomic energy, space research, and electronics.

Many things happened to the dog. His spectacular war service has made an apology for owning a dog obsolete. Today anyone can speak up with pride about his dog and ask any new acquaintance what breed he owns. It is the non-dog owner who is put on the defensive today.

Man and dog have been together, so far as is known, from the very beginning. Probably the cave-man was proud of his dog. Shepherds have always owned dogs with great pride. Hunters have valued their dogs above almost anything else they possessed.

Before World War II city dwellers still felt the need for dogs, but often felt that they must justify this need by some apology such as, "We felt a dog would be good for the kids." This, of course, was true, but it did not tell the whole story. Since the war these same people, emancipated from this complex, stand boldly by a companion who has always stood proudly by his man.

Although dogs were used by American armies in the Indian wars, dogs never became a traditional part of the armed services until World War II. There were no officer personnel trained either to set up a program or to appreciate what dogs could do for the various services. It was the civilian dog owners who, knowing how much dogs were helping both our enemies and our allies, offered their dogs which had been trained in obedience and hunting, and, in many cases, offered to go with their dogs to help.

It was fortunate that such highly responsible men and women as Messrs. Caesar and Lewis and Mmes. Erlanger and Long were selected to head up the National Dogs for Defense organization and allowed to help the Army, Coast Guard, and Marine Corps plan their training areas, training procedure and help them to choose capable training personnel.

It was my great privilege to work with these heads of Dogs for Defense and the Army, locally under Colonel F. W. Koester at the San Carlos, California, Dog Training and Reception Center. As Regional Director of Dogs for Defense, I had the unusual privilege as a civilian to help plan the training area, the housing, and even work with the directors of training on manuals to be used in all three services for such types of training as messenger service and mine detection.

My close association, especially with the directors of training, gave me an unusual opportunity to learn which of the dogs my office procured were making good in some particular field, and which dogs could not be used and why they were rejected. This gave me a new appreciation of how well a dog may do one task, and how the same dog may be useless if asked to do something for which he has inherited no aptitudes.

An amusing incident happened in the early stages of the mine detection program. (The rumor that the dogs are sacrificed in this project is completely wrong. A good mine dog is never in danger, nor is his master.) This incident, which could have been tragic if the land mines had been alive, illustrates how instinct and inherited character traits may be a handicap as well as an advantage in some types of war work.

This project was designed to find out whether the dogs who had been trained for mine detection would work efficiently if, while crawling on leash with their handler through a planted mine field, an "umbrella" of machine gun bullets was fired overhead.

All the dogs did well except one. This was an Irish water spaniel. He also did well until a sea gull swooped through the flying bullets and fell fluttering a hundred yards ahead. This dog had shown unusual aptitude for mine detection, but the fall of a fluttering bird was too much for his spaniel inheritance and he instinctively jerked free of his handler and dashed out, retrieved the bird and came back very pleased with his achievement.

Naturally he was never again trusted in mine detection, although he proved excellent in other work. Had the mines been alive both he and many of the men might have been killed by the chain of reactions such a dash across them might have set off. However, spaniel breeders over the centuries are to be complimented upon the strong impulse to retrieve that has been bred into the spaniel breeds.

During the war I screened thousands of dogs offered for service. Many of the dogs who passed our tests during the screening failed when given actual experience in some field of war work. I became increasingly aware of the inadequacy of our tests, and found some ways to improve them. I was dealing with adult dogs, mostly around twelve to eighteen months of age. I had little means of appraising their previous environments and none of knowing their inherited traits. We had dogs of all ages in my rescue group and few of them failed, although some took much longer to train than others.

At first I was of the opinion that because the rescue dogs worked with their owners they adjusted better. I think this was true. But there must be other things, too, I concluded.

There was Buddie, Russel Grant's dog who worked well with the police and fire departments even when Mr. Grant was not present. We had other dogs who would work well with any handler. There must be something that happened to a dog early in his life which made him adaptable to learning new things and willing to learn them, I decided.

Most of the rescue dogs had lived closely with their owners since they were quite young, and learned to like to do things for their masters. I began to ask the people who offered dogs for the service when they had acquired the dogs they offered, and if they had been taught to do anything for them at home. This helped make better screening possible. I explained this to myself this way: dogs who have lived happily with their owners and learned to do something have come to feel that they belong with people, and so will adjust even in an entirely strange environment, more readily to another person who expects them to work for him; they have acquired an emotional tie with human beings.

Later I was to learn that this was entirely true, how it happens, and when it happens. To my surprise, it happens much earlier in the puppy's life than I had suspected; if it does not happen then, it will never be very strong. Nothing can substitute for this experience and nothing that happens in the future will ever give the same results.

At that time I was aware of the fact that large populations of dogs with what should have been similar inheritances differed so widely that there must be some environmental influence which caused this difference. I became so concerned with this idea that I wrote to Messrs. Caesar and Lewis and asked if they had any information that would help me make better choices of the dogs I was screening.

They had no such information. I then asked if Dogs for Defense could make some kind of puppy research to see why this was happening. Our supply problems were so big and so immediate at the time that no study could be made. It was after the war when I became associated with Guide Dogs for the Blind, Inc.'s puppy program and worked with Dr. Scott that I first began to learn that many of the dogs who failed to become good war dogs might have succeeded had they had different experiences in early puppihood. All this is explained in detail in later chapters.

Early in the war, when rationing became necessary, there was some agitation for the wholesale destruction of dogs to save food. The great success of the dogs in their war effort soon hushed this clamor and reversed the public attitude toward dogs. The great number of men who learned how to train dogs in the service have provided us with some of America's outstanding dog men of today. Many have made a life work of obedience training, professional handling, breeding dogs and, in our case, of applying their knowledge to Guide Dogs for the Blind. Thousands of dog owners today train their own dogs for obedience and field trials, or just to be a better pal at home. Nothing has spurred the interest in dogs in America or caused the dog owners to learn to understand and take pride in their canine companion like World War II and its canine program. Through all this the dog's place in human progress is becoming better understood.

Seeing Eye, at Morristown, New Jersey, applied to Dogs for Defense in the early days of the war for dogs to be trained for blinded veterans. From San Francisco's Dogs for Defense office quite a few dogs were shipped to Seeing Eye. In fact, I had never thought of Guide Dogs being trained anywhere else until I met William F. Johns.

Mrs. William H. Long, Jr., National Secretary of Dogs for Defense, had written to say that she would visit my office and, if possible and convenient, she would like also to visit the San Carlos War Dog Reception and Training Center. Colonel Koester very graciously invited Mrs. Long and me to spend a day at the center to see each phase of the training program and to have lunch with the officers in charge. We were permitted to see guard dogs, scout dogs, messenger dogs and mine-detecting dogs being trained, and to discuss each type of training.

While Mrs. Long and I were being shown one group of men and dogs in training, Mrs. Long exclaimed, "Why there is Sergeant Johns," and started to get out of the car. Remembering that she was on a military reservation she turned to Colonel Koester and said, "I am sorry, but would it be possible for me to say hello to Mr. Johns. He was very active in our obedience program in the East and I should like to speak to him and tell him how proud I am to see him directing the training of a platoon here."

When Colonel Koester had the class take a rest Bill Johns came over to our car and that was the first time that he and I met.

During our trip back to San Fransicso that afternoon, Mrs. Long told me how Mr. Johns had helped so many people in the East with his knowledge of dog training and his ability to transmit this knowledge to others. She said the Army had promised Mr. Johns a Captaincy and she was sad to find that they had not done as they promised. Late in the war this oversight was partly corrected.

The next time I met Mr. Johns was when he came with his men and trucks to my office to take back a large induction of new canine candidates. We were also shipping some dogs to Seeing Eye that day.

Mr. Johns has very keen perception. "Are you supplying dogs to Seeing Eye, too?" he asked. Upon being told that we were, he told me, "The army is planning to start a Guide Dog program. If it does I would like to go over the descriptions of the dogs you have offered with you, and select enough dogs to start our training. The owners would have to be informed what we expect to do with their dogs and be willing to give them to us outright if they qualify for Guide Dogs, because they would never get them back."

A short time later the program was authorized. Mr. Johns and I spent several days picking the dogs which he believed would make good Guide Dogs. About twenty in all were selected for the first lot, and four trainers were selected to train them under Mr. Johns' instructions. The dogs were designated as "G.I. Dogs" and when they had reached the training stage where they were ready to be worked on the streets of San Francisco they created quite a sensation and many newspaper stories.

The program was very successful, but once the dogs were trained the government had no plans to use them. I had just become aware of Guide Dogs for the Blind, Inc., at this time, and arranged to have the dogs transferred to this organization, but found that they had no facilities for so many dogs. They were then offered to Seeing Eye, who accepted them. When I visited at Morristown in 1946, Mr. Ebeling said that they had found them to be very fine dogs and all but one had been assigned to a blind person.

As I said, I was just becoming aware of Guide Dogs for the Blind, Inc., which, according to the official records, was: "Organized to fill a serious need." In 1942, the United States having been plunged into another war, a small group of prominent San Francisco women who had engaged in welfare activities felt that a training school on the Pacific Coast, where Guide Dogs could be provided for men and women blinded in service, was not only desirable, but imperative. The idea behind this school was that dogs would be trained and made available to those blinded in the war whose homes were on the Pacific Coast or in the Rocky Mountain area. Thus, they would receive their training and their dogs near home. It was felt that the dogs and training should be provided free of cost to all who had given their sight for their country. Prominent among the organizers and principal contributors were Mrs. Ryer Nixon, first president, and Mrs. Nion Tucker, first vice president.

Mrs. Walter S. Heller, who was one of my mainstays in Dogs for Defense, soon became interested in Guide Dogs, too, and introduced me to it by taking my wife and me to observe a class in training. Our interest was aroused at once, and soon I was sitting in at a board of directors' meeting as an advisor. A little later I was elected to the board, and some time later to the vice presidency, which I have held ever since.

Mr. Johns' group of Guide Dog trainers made our San Francisco office their headquarters when training in the city. It was at our office that I introduced Mrs. Heller to Mr. Johns, and he was at once asked if he could not find some time to help Guide

63

Dogs for the Blind, Inc., after hours at San Carlos. This Mr. Johns did, giving a valuable boost to the program by giving freely of his time and especially of his knowledge.

After V-E Day in Europe, dogs started coming back to the training centers. Those that were not reassigned for Pacific Area service were then eligible to be returned to their homes. Unfortunately, the picture most often used in the publicity and stories about war dogs was the one where a dog was viciously attacking an enemy. This was very misleading because so very few attack dogs were trained. Most of the dogs were not given this training at all, though many would protect their handlers in any situation which called for it. There were, however, so many dogs trained for other types of service that very few dogs required a great deal of detraining to become perfectly safe to return to their owners and homes. In fact all of them had such excellent obedience training that it seemed only proper that the owners should be given some instruction in how to take advantage of this excellent training which their dogs had received. This proved to be so successful that a number of the local dogs entered into the obedience dog trials which had developed extensively during the war. Many of them received degrees and high scores in the trials.

It now became my part of the program to educate the owners. I had used obedience training to develop the rescue dogs, and now organized classes to help the owners of returning war dogs. The San Carlos War Dog Reception and Training Center now devoted its time to reconditioning the returned dogs to be friendly with everyone. They also warned the owners to avoid certain gestures and commands which might be dangerous because of the dogs' wartime training. Kindness was the motto at San Carlos.

I wrote a story about this kindness rehabilitation for the American Weekly. It was widely read and I got some very sharp criticism from those who felt that we were releasing upon the homes a lot of very dangerous animals. But it was proved here that it is all in trusting your dog and letting him know that the war is over and he can be his own self again. It was not the dog, but some boastful owner or curious neighbor, who wanted to see what the dog would do under certain circumstances, who had to be watched. We had only one bad experience and that came about by someone trying to see if the dog could be made to attack. Fortunately the results were not serious.

For four or five months I met daily with dog owners who were getting instruction in how to welcome home their canine heroes. These were wonderful students and such nice people. They were mostly people who could easily regain that rapport between man and dog which makes them an ideal team, and I began to understand why their dogs were the ones who made good as soldiers, marines and coast guardsmen. The kind of people who would not have been suited to receive back a dog had mostly spoiled their dogs by neglect or indifference. It was their dogs who had been rejected in training. These latter people expect an animal to work like a machine. It is terrible that some people have never learned about the wonders of nature, of animals and plants and even minerals.

Our present civilization needs more dogs in the homes while children are very young. Almost anyone can have a dog, and this in itself helps us to appreciate other species. An experience such as we had with Skookie can develop in almost anyone a deep appreciation for other members of the animal kingdom. After all, we belong to the animal kingdom, too.

Skookie had proved to be just as fine an obedience trial dog as he had been a hunter, a field trial dog and a rescue dog. He helped me show the owners of the returning war dogs what their dogs had learned to do by illustrating how they would obey all the obedience commands for them as well as for their service trainers. When I taught the owners what their dogs had learned to do I also showed them how the chain collars to which the dogs had become accustomed were properly put on. There is a proper way so that when the leash is slack the collar will open and hang loosely around the dog's neck. If the collar is put on the other way it remains tight and chokes the dog. Skookie would help me illustrate this by sitting on my desk and holding his head up so everyone in the room could see the proper way to put the collar on.

Skookie was doing just fine in everything and then tragedy struck.

In Obedience he won his Companion Dog title with high scores. He was exemplary in his Rescue Dog work. In the field he was doing great. While still a puppy he placed third in stiff Open All Age Competition.

This one was a thriller. He had done well under the first judge. Under the second judge the course lay through a heavy growth of weeds which were higher than my head and so thick that I could not see Skookie at all. After walking into this cover for about twenty yards I realized that I would not see him again for some time. To compensate I tried to figure about when he should be at the end of each cast from one side of the course to the other, a distance of about forty yards. Each time he should turn to cover the course in the opposite direction, according to my calculations, I gave the turn signal by tweeting twice on the whistle. I had been doing this for some little time when the judge turned to me and demanded, "Where is your dog?"

"Right out there where he should be, tweet, tweet," I replied.

"Well maybe you see him, but I don't," he retorted.

A few minutes later we came to lower cover and sure enough there was Skookie, right where he should be and making his turn on my tweets.

Just then a big cock pheasant flew up as he dashed into some heavy cover. Skookie at once hupped (sat) in his tracks in the cover while the guns just out of the high stuff blazed away at the fast-flying rooster. The shots only crippled the bird and he came down way out, running.

"Can your dog make that retrieve?" the judge asked me.

It was a long fall and the bird was unquestionably a runner, but I had great confidence in my dog, so I replied, "Why, of course he can."

For ten minutes we could see the grass and weeds waving this way and that as Skookie followed the trail of the running pheasant, then the bird leaped high in the air for a takeoff, but Skookie was right up there with him and caught him in mid-air. Back through the punishing cover came the pup with the big bird in his mouth. As he neared us we could see that the bird was fighting him every step of the way, picking with his sharp beak and scratching with his long spurs. This was a wild bird which had wandered onto the course, fully grown and very strong, but Skookie delivered it softly to my hand.

I gave the fighting bird to the judge while I wiped the blood from the wounds he inflicted on Skookie's face. As soon as I was released from further competition I picked Skookie up and carried him in my arms back to our car.

An interesting sequel happened a week later at the field trial held at Woodland. Up to that day Skookie had always been spectacular at making quick pickups and fast direct retrieves to my hand. At Woodland I was puzzled when he took a long time to pick a bird up and then came back to me very slowly. His head was held high, but I was puzzled about what he was bringing. So was the judge.

"For God's sake, what kind of a retrieve do you call that?" the judge asked me.

What Skookie was presenting to me was the tail and kicking feet of a big pheasant. He had doubled the head back on the bird's breast and was carrying the bird by holding the head and neck and part of the breast in his mouth. He had made sure that this bird could not peck and spur him.

There are times I wish I had some of that wonderful instinct that our animals have. Too bad they cannot reason.

Shortly after this, one morning as I was leaving for school Skookie came to the door with Juanita to tell me goodbye. As she stroked his lovely coat she stopped suddenly. "Why, Skookie has a lot of bumps under his skin," she said.

I stroked his coat and then examined the bumps. We had never seen anything like them. That afternoon I took him to our veterinarian. He was not happy with what he saw and suggested that I show Skookie to another veterinarian for an opinion. The second doctor recommended a third. The third consulted with the other two and told me that he was quite sure that Skookie had skin cancer, but he asked that I take him to the University of California Medical School. A biopsy confirmed the diagnosis. At that time there was no known treatment for this disease.

At the hospital they told me that they had had some unusual experiences with the disease. In one case after a simple biopsy the disease disappeared and that now, two years later, it had not returned. Often the disease ran a short time and then disappeared only to come back months later with killing force. The cause or a cure were unknown.

After the biopsy the lumps gradually disappeared and we took courage. A year later they reappeared and this time they got constantly worse. Skookie seemed to feel no pain from them. He hunted just as well as ever and loved every minute of it. He made two legs on his Companion Dog Excellent title still with high scores and could have made the other except that I did not want his many admirers to see how this beautiful dog's coat was dry and bumpy. I wanted them to remember him in his glory.

One afternoon I came home from work and Juanita told me Skookie had not been his merry self all day. She had stayed in the basement near him, but he seemed restless.

As soon as I arrived I tried to coax him to his bed, but he lay on the cool concrete floor and wanted to stay there. So I sat on the floor beside him.

I guess he had just waited for me to come home.

CHAPTER V

The Dignity of Being an Individual

When my fellow members of the board of directors of Guide Dogs for the Blind, Inc., learned that I had been honored by being invited to serve on the Obedience Rules Committee by the American Kennel Club, and that I would be in New York in June, 1946, they asked me if I would take a little time while in the East to see if we could learn what was known about testing puppies to determine what kind of dogs they would be when they grew up.

We knew that the Department of Agriculture, at the national experimental farm at Beltsville, Maryland, had had a puppy program to study herding dogs. Beltsville is very near Washington D.C.

I wrote to Dr. Walter M. Dawson, who was in charge of the program. Dr. Dawson very kindly made an appointment for me to spend a day with him and his associates at the farm. I flew directly to Washington and took a bus out to the farm. I was disappointed to find no dogs there. I remembered that we had a War Dog Training Center on the farm while I was regional director of Dogs for Defense. I naturally presumed that the government had in some way used Dr. Dawson's project to further the War Dog program. I learned that this was not the case. Instead, as soon as the war started, his project had been declared surplus, his dogs had been auctioned off at any price they could

When the especially bred and raised Guide Dog puppy grows up to a size which will fit this harness, he will have a 94% chance of making a good guide dog. Most good dogs have a 20% to 25% chance of making good as guides.

A guide dog for the blind must be so reliable that his mistress will experience the independence of a sighted person, freedom of motion and a life free from the apprehension of impending danger. Here Miss Magdalene Phillips and her guide dog, Tanya, feel the wind and the sun in their hair as they stroll over the hills. Miss Phillips is PBX operator at Guide Dogs for the Blind, Inc., and teaches others to operate a braille switchboard. She also conducts tours so expertly that guests at the school cannot believe she is blind.

These 12-weeks-old German shepherd puppies adjust immediately to the 4-H Club Members who will raise them. From 8 to 12 weeks, each Thursday they have been socialized while given their tests by the group of volunteer women at Guide Dogs for the Blind, Inc., San Rafael, Calif. They get approximately 30 minutes of socialization once a week. Otherwise they are kennel raised. At 12 weeks they are heeling on lead, retrieving, sitting, coming on command. These puppies are passed from one tester to another for different experiences. Each tester makes a point of being especially friendly, of praising profusely, and petting the puppy. A test is done individually, the puppy taught self reliance and pride in achievement. The dignity of being an individual is impressed upon him. No food is ever given as a reward. Punishment is not used in training, nor tolerated.

get for them, and his training area turned into a swine breeding experimental yard. I learned that Dr. Dawson's report had been set up in type at the government printing office to be printed and distributed for the benefit of all of us interested in better dog breeding, but I understand it was never printed.

What was most disheartening was that Dr. Dawson had assembled, after great care, a colony of the dogs which we used to have on the farm and called shepherds, English shepherds, or farm collies. This was a breed which most of us old enough to remember them think of as America's greatest contribution to the canine breeds. He was a fine upstanding dog, usually black and white, rather squarely built and usually weighing around fifty pounds. He could be sent for the cows or would take a message to the folks working in the field. He was a wonderful all-purpose dog. He was greatly sought after by the armed forces, but hard to find. The glamour of imported breeds had swept America and we had cross-bred him to almost anything that came from Europe until, during the war, what we got in his stead were mostly cross-breds. C-Bs, we called them on our records. These were the dogs that had been sold by our government for a song while hundreds of volunteers were begging for this kind of dog for service to our country.

This made me especially sad a few days later when I visited Seeing Eye. Here Mr. Ebeling told me that they had had a few English shepherds which trained so well that they wished they had saved them for breeding instead of altering them and using them for guides. He strongly recommended that if Guide Dogs could find any of these of good quality that they obtain them and try to rebuild the breed. While he liked the German shepherds and Labradors they were using, he was most impressed with the English shepherd. Dr. Dawson, too, had found them excellent. Dr. Leon Whitney, of Orange, Connecticut, told me that of all breeds he would recommend for guides, the English shepherd would head the list. (I have known Dr. Whitney for many years and have no patience with his detractors. He spent many years working in experimental testing and breeding for one of America's most honored universities and has contributed impressively to the betterment of dogs.)

71

Dr. Whitney also told me of some blind people on Long Island whom he used to see using fox terriers as Guide Dogs when he was a boy. They had a harness on the dog and a broom handle which they held while the dogs guided them. So, as much as Fortunate Field contributed to the guide dog movement, and it was a most significant contribution, it would appear that, like most great advances in any field, there existed someone who had done some exploration in advance.

The testing which Dr. Dawson had done had been with English shepherds, border collies and pulik. The experiment had been to select the strains from those who showed the most natural ability in herding, to breed for this quality, to learn how to select for this quality while they were quite young, and to cross-breed these dogs to determine how the character traits were inherited and whether or not there was a new vitalization of these traits in the cross-breds. Although he had completed the five-year experiment he had been authorized to make, he felt that another five years was needed to arrive at definite enough conclusions to make his experiment important. This seems to be the experience of all of us, that ten to twenty years are needed in a puppy research program to make it valid. In five years you are about well started and probably have no valid conclusions. Dr. Dawson used sheep mostly with his dogs, although I believe he did use some other stock and possibly turkeys. He made the direct approach to his problem even more practically than we can at Guide Dogs. He started his experiments with very young puppies and carried them through the development of a puppy herding instinct to adulthood.

Mr. Ebeling told me that at Seeing Eye they had worked at their breeding program mostly by using known quality for breeding, breeding dogs and bitches which they first trained to determine their quality as guide dogs. They also had their foundation stock, of course, from Fortunate Field where a large experimental program in breeding and selection had taken place before Seeing Eye was established. I liked the dogs I saw there very much, especially the shepherds.

Dr. Whitney had experimented with many breeds, but his best known experiments have been his cross-bred bloodhound ex

English bull terrier. He told me that he got the most intelligent dogs and most interesting dogs from this combination. He felt that they were highly useful. Of course, when he bred these two breeds together he got the useful ones, but when he bred these cross-breds to similar cross-breds he got a most undesirable and unpredictable assortment. (I had not at this time been properly indoctrinated in the use of cross-breeding and was rather upset by the deliberate breeding of two such distinct breeds as blood-hounds and bull terriers at Dr. Whitney's, and of the border collie and the puli at Beltsville. I was to get my real shock years later when I found the cross-breeding of basenjis and cocker spaniels at Bar Harbor. There is a need for this sort of thing in any scientific research into the inherited traits of animal life.)

To most Americans, and especially to the American Kennel Club, cross-breeding is not to be thought of. To the European it it not looked upon in the same way we look at it. The boxer and the Doberman pinscher are manufactured breeds from Germany. The English long used related breeds together. For years the large spaniels were shown as springer spaniels in Eng-land and the smaller ones from the same litter as cocker spaniels. For years American springer field trial men looked for a certain prepotent dog in the most sought-after pedigrees. That dog was registered as a cocker spaniel.

It has been important to learn these things and I think they should be more generally understood, but of course what I was searching for was not some way to start a new breed, but how to select, from the breeds which we were then using, the dogs who would become Guide Dogs and especially how to breed strains of these breeds who would be reliable producers of Guide Dogs. It was many years later that I came to understand how the use of the cross-breeding programs had contributed knowledge which would aid in this search.

I talked with Monty Lewis, who had developed his own strain of very successful American cocker spaniel field trial dogs. He had found what he wanted and then had used closely related dogs from those lines to continue his strain.

In each case I found that everyone with whom I talked always had some ideal dog, or nearly ideal dog, which they had used, and had preserved his or her genes in the lines they developed. This was to prove true with us later when Mr. Johns gave us the German shepherd, Frank of Ledge Acres.

Everyone I talked with shared their knowledge of dogs with me without any reservation, but when I asked them how I should go about testing Guide Dog puppies to find out which ones would be almost sure to fail and which would be almost sure to succeed, no one was able to give me the formula I sought. Later, when we actually started puppy testing at San Rafael, I wrote each of them about what we were doing and what problems we had and each gave me the best advice he could. Many of their suggestions were excellent and were incorporated in one way or another into our testing program.

As an example: Mr. Lewis wrote that he thought we should have some training tests. He suggested retrieving. We added heel on leash, come, sit and fetch. Fetch has proved to be one of our best predictors. What each contributed helped us to straighten out our thinking and gave us great encouragement. Before Mr. Lewis made his suggestion about training we had been using a new experience each week, laboring under the impression that we could best detect aptitude traits by the way a puppy reacted to his first experience with a new situation. We have retained the new-experience tests, but both Dr. Scott and I have found that puppies test better when they also have some training. Since then I have had the opportunity to talk this over with psychologists doing similar experiments with children and they, too, have found that the most reliable tests are those associated with some training. Our most reliable new-experience tests have to do with how a puppy reacts to what he sees, such as moving vehicles, obstructions, overhangs, and pedestrians. Previous training in heeling makes these tests possible.

With all this valuable information, I had still to meet a person with experience in puppy testing who had had similar enough experience with puppies to what I felt we would be doing, and on whom I could call for advice. I had heard that there was a behavior program at the Roscoe B. Jackson Memorial Laboratory, Bar Harbor, Maine, where dogs were being studied to learn about human behavior. So I asked Mr. Henry D. Bixby, who was at that time the executive vice-president of the American Kennel Club, whether he knew if they would be able to help me. He thought they would.

I went to Bar Harbor.

I remember particularly my first visit with Dr. Scott. He had been working on his animal behavior project at Hamilton Station only ten months. I could see that he was very busy and I felt that I was imposing and said so, but he insisted on showing me the laboratory and in learning why I had come four thousand miles to see him.

"If you can stay this evening, so we can sit down and be more relaxed, maybe we can help you get started on your project," he suggested.

I was so fascinated that had he asked me to stay a week I would have agreed.

"Meanwhile, maybe you would like to observe some of our work. Why don't you go out in the field and observe some of the puppies with Dr. Hall?"

"Follow this path, take the branch to the left, after about a hundred yards you will see a five-foot board fence on your right. Please keep on the main path and do not approach the fence. When you are well past where the fence ends your path will turn right. It will lead you to a tall tree. Up in the tree you will see a man looking through field glasses and taking notes. Climb up to where he is working, but be very quiet."

I followed the path with mixed emotions. I had come to ask Dr. Scott how to test puppies. For awhile I had thought he was going to tell me. I had traveled across a continent to see a man about dog problems because I was up a tree with dog troubles, now this man was sending me deep into the woods to climb another tree.

After I had climbed the tree and made, literally, a "nodding acquaintance" with Dr. Hall, I was doubly perplexed, for, look as hard as I could, I did not see any puppies anywhere. Instead, before me lay a large field of uncut grass. It and the adjoining fields were all surrounded by high board fences, none of which seemed to even have a gate. There was a little box structure in the center of each field.

Dr. Hall handed me the glasses and directed me by gesture to look. After a long while I did locate a few grown dogs, one in each field, and in some fields there were two. It took the help of Dr. Hall to find the puppies.

As I sat there, I wondered if I, too, would have to sit in a tree and study puppies in a hay field to learn to pick puppies capable of becoming Guide Dogs. Well, that has proved to be unnecessary in our case, but during the fourteen years since I climbed that tree to look down on those fields of waving grass I have come to have a very high regard for the studies which have been made there, and the findings which have proved to be so valuable to our own evaluation of puppies. It has taken the knowledge which Drs. Scott and Hall, and others since, have gathered from those boarded-up acre plots to explain much that we have learned, and has enabled us to apply what we have learned to produce puppies which will become good Guide Dogs.

The photograph of the boarded-up acre fields in this book shows clear areas on two sides of the fields. In 1956 the woods grew right up to the fences, and the dogs lived in as nearly primitive states as is possible in any form of restraint.

Late that afternoon Dr. Hall and I climbed down from the tree. Frankly, I couldn't say I had learned anything. On our way back to the laboratory, when we were out of hearing distance of the dogs in the field, Dr. Hall explained that in each field were a mother and her puppies. In some fields both the mother and the father were with their puppies. Each family was pure bred, but in each field was a different breed. Some of the breeds then being studied were beagles, wire fox terriers and Scottish terriers.

"We are trying to simulate a condition in which dogs might live if they were suddenly reverted to their natural, undomestic state. We want to see how a dog mother raises her puppies when she is not being supervised by people. We want to learn how dogs conduct their own social organization. We want to know whether dogs raised in this environment will behave like normal dogs when they are associated with people in a man-dog team.

"These dogs have no contact with anyone except the man who brings them their daily food and water, and he takes great care not to show them any affection, or even to speak to them. He simply moves in and out as mechanically as possible. All socializing behaviors are avoided," Dr. Hall told me.

"What are you finding out?" I wanted to know.

"We aren't learning much about puppies under four weeks of age. They all seem to stay right in their nest boxes. At about four weeks of age most of them venture out for a little look around. Occasionally, we see one between twenty-one and twenty-eight days of age who has ventured outside, but none of these wander very far from the kennel. When they start coming out they play around close to their box in puppy fashion. They rarely go far away from home base until they are about twelve weeks old. Then they start exploring more and more as individuals and in pairs. Their social organization seems to be very much the same as that of litters raised in a home or a kennel; that is, they behave just about the same toward each other whether they are raised in a field without human supervision or they are raised in a home or a kennel with supervision.

"The attitude of these field-raised puppies, especially around twelve weeks of age and older, toward people is an entirely different matter. This lack of social adjustment to people, which we have deliberately arranged, may have very significant results. We haven't gone very far with this, but we can see that this may be very important," Dr. Hall felt.

Looking back fourteen years, that last paragraph strikes home with great force. By 1948, using the puppies from the boarded-up acre fields and those from the nursery for contrasts in the studies of socialization, Dr. Scott was able to name the critical periods in the lives of the puppies. These periods which are being more closely defined as more study is being given them may be the most important discovery about dogs (and children) in the twentieth century.

When Dr. Hall and I arrived at the Hamilton Station Laboratory office we found Dr. Scott ready to leave.

"I have to go over to the main laboratory, seven or eight miles from here. Why don't you go with me? We may catch Dr. Little before he leaves for New York. If not, you can browse around and get some idea of what goes on over there, while I attend to some business. Then, we will pick up Mrs. Scott and meet Dr. Hall for dinner," Dr. Scott invited.

And it was thus that I saw Bar Harbor with its formal gardens on estates that ran from the waterfront up and over the dome-shaped hills of Mt. Desert Island. This was the summer home and playground of many of America's most wealthy families. I saw the old Main Laboratory, which, together with so many of the estates, was to be burned to the ground in the holocaust a few months later. The fire crested and burned so rapidly that only human beings and a few wild animals were able to escape by fleeing to the water. Fortunately, Hamilton Station and most of the estates along the shore in Bar Harbor were spared.

In 1946 we had no premonition of a catastrophe greater than being unable to breed dogs who would train better for Guide Dogs than those we had produced to date.

Back in Bar Harbor, Dr. and Mrs. Scott and Dr. Hall and I enjoyed a delicious shore dinner while we discussed my problems. There were times when the discussion between Drs. Scott and Hall got into realms far beyond me, for I had had little training in this field. I had had a lot of courses in education, sociology and kindred subjects, and a very little psychology, but the things they talked about that night in the animal behavior field were often completely out of my experience and training.

So I thought then. During the years that we have worked together, I have found that dog people and psychologists talk about the same things; they just have different vocabularies. This is unfortunate because often each has valuable information for the other. It is too bad that there is not a better means of communication. I find that both often wonder where to turn for facts they need. Well, in this book the vocabulary of the kennel predominates, but the facts learned by important scientists are revealed. We have tried to make it just as trustworthy as a scientific paper without too many, "It can therefore be assumed," or, "The hypothesis is . . ." In the few instances where the experiment has not been brought to what seems to be a logical conclusion we state plainly that this is still in the experimental stage.

"I am not sure that we can help you very much," Dr. Scott told me with that caution I have since learned to associate with any advice you get from a true scientist. "You are starting on a rather new field of research. So far as I know few, if any, practical approaches have been made to the selection of puppies. I doubt if anyone has as yet arrived at a solution of how to predict, with any degree of accuracy, what the behavior of an adult dog will be by tests given to puppies.

"I can see that you are looking for a very special dog. It is just possible that it will be almost, if not entirely, impossible to devise a set of tests which will give you the right results. You may find that you will have to be satisfied with twenty-five per cent success in training dogs for such exacting work.

"There seems to be enough possibility that you might succeed to justify trying. What you learn may be of considerable value to others doing research in animal behavior, whether you succeed in your project or not."

At this point I was getting pretty discouraged. Since then I have come to understand that failure may be more important than success in a scientific experiment. It may contribute more to world knowledge.

At the moment I was looking for a road sign which would read, "This Way To Success." I had a problem; "How can we get better dogs for Guide Dogs?" I was looking for a direct route, but it wasn't going to be that easy.

"There are some indications," Dr. Scott was saying, "that there are periods in a puppy's life when you can do certain things for him better than you can ever do them again. And there are probably times when whatever you do for him will have little effect or make much of an impression.

"You are planning to test your puppies. You will have to select an age when the tests should begin and one when they can be terminated. I believe that Dr. Hall will agree with me, I think you cannot do much testing, if any, before the puppy is four weeks of age. By twelve or at most sixteen weeks of age you should have completed your tests. It is likely that somewhere in this bracket of ages you will find the most ideal time for puppy testing." Dr. Hall nodded his approval.

On our trip over to the Main Laboratory I had learned from Dr. Scott that Dr. Hall, a prominent psychologist, had taken a year off from his duties with Western Reserve University to help Dr. Scott set up the Animal Behavior Laboratory program at Hamilton Station.

"Even if Mr. Pfaffenberger gets no positive predictability from his tests, I believe that the socialization which the puppies will receive while being tested will probably improve the trainability of the dogs enough to justify the time it will take. He will find that socialization of the puppies at this age will materially increase the percentage of Guide Dogs that his school will get from dogs of a quality equal to the dogs they are now training. I can even envision that he might double the number that will prove to be trainable, just by the socialization," Dr. Hall predicted.

"By socialization we mean the process of forming relationships between dogs and human beings. It appears that these relationships may be established quite normally and naturally with many animals if the attempt is made during certain periods in the animal's life. That is why we have suggested certain ages for the puppy tests. It will be some time before we know just what these ages are and what is significant about them, but it is quite certain that they range somewhere within the limits we have given you," Dr. Scott explained. "If you consider the relationship of a dog to his master you will see that it closely parallels that of a child to a parent. To get the best results the socialization which creates this relationship must start as soon as the dog is old enough to begin accepting the relationship."

"What sort of tests do you suggest would be best for us to use?" I asked. "I was pleased to note that you do not use mazes in your tests. To me a maze is good for a mouse or a rat, but it just is not natural for a puppy. I feel that our tests for a dog should be geared to his natural ability, to things he would do naturally. I would like to test the puppies in their ability to do some of the things they will do when grown. With sporting dogs we try them out on pheasant wings and things which should naturally interest them."

I had shown my feeling about this so strongly that I was slightly embarrassed when Dr. Scott smiled at Dr. Hall and asked, "Shall we tell him?"

Dr. Hall laughed, "The fact is we do have some maze tests,

one or two. Actually, both of us believe with you in principle, but the average animal behaviorist is so accustomed to mazes that if we did not have one or two here they would think we did not know anything about testing animals. The fact is, the maze has its place even in testing a puppy's reactions. You can learn a good deal about his ingenuity, intelligence and persistence, or will to do, if you provide the proper incentive for him to solve the maze."

(In our tests at Guide Dogs we have never used a maze, except a small plywood panel behind which a ten-week-old puppy is placed before being called by the tester. He can back out or wiggle his way so as to turn around. We use it to see how eager he is to come when called.)

"You are welcome to copies of our tests and the small amount of published materials we have been able to get out so far," Dr. Scott told me. "I suspect, however, that you can work out better tests for your purpose than those we have."

"Tell us something about what a Guide Dog has to do," Dr. Hall prompted.

When I explained how a Guide Dog works and what he must do to be safe and what he cannot do, he wanted to know just exactly what most of the dogs did wrong who failed to qualify and why what they did made us sure that they were unsafe to lead the blind.

Both Dr. Hall and Dr. Scott agreed that our tests should come from some sort of experiences which would as nearly simulate what a Guide Dog has to do as possible, especially those things which make him safe, also that we should try to devise tests which would show the character traits which seemed most likely to fail a Guide Dog. Detecting the useful and the dangerous inherited traits should substantially improve our method of selection, they felt.

The early experience of the puppies seemed to be almost an obsession with both of them. It got me thinking about some of my personal experiences.

"You both seem to put a lot of stress on the importance of early experience in a puppy's life," I said. "It has never occured to me that the age when a puppy is socialized should be so important, and yet my own experience should have told me that it is."

Both Dr. Scott and Dr. Hall showed interest in what I was saying, so I told them about Skookie.

"For nearly fifteen years I have been raising and training cocker spaniels in field trials as a hobby. Early in 1940 we had a one-puppy litter. Having no other pups at the time I started to train this little fellow at about four weeks of age. I had not realized until now that the time in his life when he received his first training may have been such a big factor in his phenomenal success. Skookie had acquired the dignity of being an individual very early in his life.

"I guess I have been thinking of this early training, but subconsciously. Come to think of it, the next year we had two litters and I selected one from one litter and two from the other and gave them the same start that I had given the lone puppy. The only difference was that we came East when the puppies were only three months old and, because they were doing so well, we asked our friends, the John Crosbys, to keep them for us while we were away. Ten weeks later when we came home they said they were sorry that they had not had much time to keep them in training. When we took the puppies home, however, they remembered everything I had taught them and worked just fine," I concluded.

Both Scott and Hall seemed to feel that what I had told them was important and I decided that when I came home, if there were tests to be given puppies at Guide Dogs for the Blind, Inc., they would begin when the puppies were quite young.

It was not until 1948 that Dr. Scott announced the definite critical periods in the life of puppies. These are so definite that he can tell a breeder just when and when not to do certain things, and the breeder can be sure that if he follows Dr. Scott's advice he will profit by doing so. What this means to our human babies has not yet been fully evaluated. That there is an interest in what we are learning is shown by the fact that The Journal of Genetic Psychology printed some of our findings in 1959, Vol. 95, pp. 145–155.

CHAPTER VI

We Make Our Own Puppy Tests

We found ourselves entering into an entirely new field of aptitude tests. Dr. Dawson was the only person we had found actually testing puppies for practical dog use. He could give his puppies sheep-herding experience and grade them on their behavior. We could not let little puppies lead blind people. We had to find out, some other way, whether they had inherited character traits which would make them suitable as Guide Dogs.

To our dismay, we found that after we had developed tests based upon giving our puppies a simulated experience of what they would have to do as Guide Dogs, some of our highest test puppies were among those who failed in training. What was even more disconcerting was that in training these same puppies, now adults, showed all the good qualities their tests had predicted. Their failure was due to the fact that as Guide Dogs they would not take the responsibility of making a decision for their master in dangerous situations such as heavy traffic and dangerous obstructions. In such a case the dog must make the decision whether to obey his master's command or to refuse to obey. The master must accept his dog's decision.

It was many years before we learned that this matter of self-confidence is instilled in the puppy by what happens to it very early in its life. It came about through the timing in environmental changes, so slight that we were hardly aware they were taking place. A chapter is devoted to the findings of this very important discovery.

One thing we had was plenty of room for improvement. Our school had set a quota of fifty Guide Dogs a year. The nearest it came during the first five years was nine Guide Dogs each in 1945 and 1946. During 1946 our trainers had put one hundred and nine dogs in training to produce the nine Guide Dogs—a little more than eight per cent success. In recent years our selected breeding stock produces from ninety to ninety-five per cent Guide Dogs while our experimental new strains are producing about sixty-five per cent Guide Dogs. These will improve as we are able to select the individuals who have the desired qualities to perpetuate the strains.

At the time that I went East to visit Beltsville Station, Seeing Eye, Hamilton Station, and other authorities, the Guide Dogs for the Blind School was still located at Los Gatos. We had purchased eleven and a half acres of pasture land near San Rafael and started construction of kennels at the new site, but just following the war materials and labor were so hard to get that the building went slowly. When I returned I found that we would not have any puppies at the new location to test until the next spring.

I was just at the stage of being reassigned to classes for the time I had been excused by the Board of Education for the Dogs for Defense work. Since I had a full day's schedule and classes three nights a week, I was at a loss to see how I could possibly start any tests. Fortunately, the superintendent of schools and the board had been pleased with both the Rescue Dog program and the Dogs for Defense. I explained what I had learned and told them about my time problem. The matter was taken up with the state board of education and I was told I could organize an adult class in animal behavior, especially puppies, if I found that at least twenty persons were sufficiently interested to attend classes.

Not only twenty, but more than thirty, enrolled, and attended very well. This large number had two effects: it brought in a number of persons who had had the testing and measurement of children as a part of their college training, and also four or five who had worked in private or government offices where

Larry Rees photo

Like a car from a blind side road, the cart comes from behind a bush into the path of the 12-weeks-old Chesapeake Bay retriever led by Mrs. A. R. Lubersky. Notice how close Mrs. Sidney Clokie has run the cart to Mrs. Lubersky's toes. The puppy was at Mrs. Lubersky's left side when the cart came out. The puppy has gotten well out of the way, but has not become panicky. It has stopped to size up the cart. A puppy too dull to get out of the way or frightened would be rejected as a guide dog prospect. As an adult its reactions to new situations will be very much the same as those shown at 12 weeks. A puppy like this, when grown, can be trained to control its responses so as to protect the blind from traffic and other dangers.

85

Bonnie Winter, a puppy tester, is training a 10-weeks-old German shepherd puppy to heel. Notice how the puppy is taught to "lead-out." A Guide Dog must walk slightly ahead of the blind person so as to pull on the harness. By starting the puppy to heel leading-out it develops the correct habit for later training.

Jon Brenneis photo

In the wire puppy pen an 11-weeks-old German shepherd puppy is tested for temperament. The wire sides give the score keepers in the background a clear view. The wire bottom is easy to keep clean, in case of accidental voiding by the puppy. Good temperament is a must for Guide Dogs.

Jon Brenneis photo

they had given such tests. The group that wanted to take part when we started our tests the following March was so large we had to improvise things for them to do; we put in some tests that we did not feel had much value at the time, but in some cases they proved to be among our best tests. From this we learned to always explore everything we could possibly investigate. In research one cannot afford to have a preconceived point of view about what one can learn.

To determine what kind of tests we could give which, we hoped, would reveal the puppy's inherited character traits so that we could tell if he had any of the faults which would prevent him from becoming a Guide Dog, we first asked our instructors at Guide Dogs to make a list of the reasons why dogs failed. Here is the list they gave us:

1. Mentally dull, does not take an interest in his lessons.
2. Ear sensitivity dull, slow to react to sounds.
3. Body sensitivity dull, does not seem to feel corrections.
4. Smarty, thinks it knows everything already.
5. Ear sensitivity too acute, shies at noises.
6. Too body sensitive, constantly afraid of corrections.
7. Has a fawning personality, always pays more attention to his trainer, personally, than to what he is being taught.
8. Afraid of persons or moving objects, especially wheeled objects.
9. Not aware of persons or moving wheeled objects, will run into them or allow them to run into him.
10. Bites, especially because he is afraid.
11. Too stubborn to be taught.
12. Lacks stability, will act one way one day and, under similar circumstances, will act entirely differently another.

According to the tests we devised, we found that in many of the litters that we were then breeding, few if any of the puppies got a passing grade. We wondered if the tests were too severe, but about fifteen months later, when these same puppies were trained, ninety per cent of those who failed in the tests failed in training. It was necessary at first to raise all the puppies and train them so that we could evaluate the tests. This meant that the people who raised puppies for us, as well as the trainers, were disappointed. While it is necessary to have controls in any type of testing, we were gradually able to reduce the controls to about twenty-five per cent, and, later, to a much lower percentage. Now we use very few.

The puppies who passed the tests did not show as consistent results in training, so we were taking losses which had nothing to do with the dog's ability to make a Guide Dog—losses due to such accidents as those which caused physical disability and distemper teeth. This was true because there was not yet close enough cooperation between the training staff and the testing volunteers. We, as volunteers, had no access to the training records and were only told if the dog made a Guide Dog or if it failed. Later, when we developed uniform methods of scoring in the tests and in training, and kept a comparative chart where all the records on each puppy are kept in parallel columns to show how the same dog was scored in each type of test and the same type of training, we began to get a more accurate picture. This was when we began to realize how many good dogs failed because they "would not take responsibility."

The tests we developed to discover the puppies who had inherited the character traits which would show up in the twelve faults listed by the trainers were:

1. A series of experiences with something new, such as a flashlight shining toward them, a mirror where they could see themselves, an object dragged along at the end of a string, a sheet of white letterhead paper waved in front of them. "Curiosity is a sign of intelligence."

2. A police whistle blown, a door chime sounded, a buzzer buzzed and an automobile horn blown, each out of the puppy's sight. If he showed that he heard it that was satisfactory. If he tried to locate the source of the sound that was excellent.

3. We found that we had to reverse our body sensitivity tests. We started with stroking the puppy's tail. We got little reaction. We found that body sensitivity increases quite rapidly from eight weeks to twelve weeks of age. So we started with pinching the puppy's ear between the ball of the thumb and the forefinger, squeezing with the ball of the thumb and finger between the puppies toes, pushing down on the collar to attempt to cause the

puppy to lie down, and then stroking the puppy's tail, in that order, in successive weeks. This gave us the most accurate tests on body sensitivity. If a puppy reacted, complained but forgave the tester, he was considered an ideal puppy in his sensitivity tests.

4. The smarty puppy tries to take the leash away from you. He goes off on some other errand when you are testing him and gives little attention to what you are doing.

5. The puppy who startles when any of the sounds we use are made will be too ear sensitive. We tried using guns at thirty paces. The sound of the 36-calibre pistol at this distance was seldom noticed by a puppy; but it set the mothers crazy, so we gave it up.

6. A puppy that cowers when any of the body tests are given, and shows undue pain, tries to get away, or does not forgive the tester, has too much body sensitivity.

7. Since we have been using the training tests which I will outline next, we have found the fawners. They try to get your attention so they will not be required to do what you want them to do. This puppy is easily spoiled and very few puppy raisers can bring him to his senses, so that he will learn to like to do things for his master.

8. It used to be that we often found puppies who, when approached by a little two-wheeled cart we use in this test, would try to pull their head out of their collar to get away. Some would urinate and some would defecate from fear. Some were as afraid of a pedestrian approaching. These puppies will never make reliable Guide Dogs because when they are confronted with unusual situations they will panic.

9. The opposite type of fault is the puppy who will blunder into a pedestrain or let a vehicle run into him.

10. The puppy who becomes frightened by the approach of a moving vehicle or a person will usually develop into a dog so shy that it will bite when it is frightened. There is another type of biter. He will bite the tester to avoid taking a test, and he will grow up to be a biter. In the early days I had one puppy, ten weeks of age, tear my trousers nearly off me. We kept him until he was grown. There was always someone who thought

that he or she could make a good dog out of him. In training he bit every trainer who worked with him and had to be destroyed.

One of our best tests for temperament is discovering the natural attitude of the young puppy to people. Our puppies are all kennel-raised and have very little socialization, except on Thursdays when they each have about a half hour of socialization while being tested by many different people. For this test we place the puppy in a wire-bottomed pen with wire sides about three and a half feet high. On the eighth week one person, a stranger to the puppy, approaches the pen and stands looking down on the puppy talking to it. It should pay attention and show friendliness. The ninth week strangers approach from all four sides of the pen and stand allowing the puppy to look them over and show interest. The tenth week the puppy is led near a stranger who jumps right at the puppy. It should show neither fear nor anger. By using these tests we have eliminated almost all our shy dogs from our program. We no longer have biters.

11. The puppy who is too stubborn to be trained will show this in our trainability tests, which will be explained.

12. It is a little hard to tell whether a puppy is acting differently because it is unstable or because it is not feeling well on a certain Thursday, but over the five Thursdays we get a rather good picture of the puppy's willingness and regularity.

Many of the men we consulted on our first trip East helped us after we got started in our tests by reading our reports and making suggestions of ways of improving our tests. The tests I have described in this chapter are the ones we use today, and have been greatly refined from the original tests. Some tests have been added and some have been dropped.

A good example of the way the practical dog men and women helped us improve our tests is illustrated by a letter received from the late Mr. A. M. "Monty" Lewis. He wrote that he felt that we would improve our tests very much if we added some training tests. He especially recommended retrieving. This was added, together with heel, come and sit. We had little expectation that fetch was significant at the time.

In 1954, when we made our first thorough analysis of any of our tests, I was working with Dr. John L. Fuller at Hamilton

Station, Bar Harbor. While checking to see if any of the tests showed more significance in predicting which puppy would make a Guide Dog than others, Dr. Fuller asked if I had noticed how many puppies who passed the fetch test became Guide Dogs. I said I had not. Then we checked other tests and we saw that the puppies who became Guide Dogs almost invariably had good fetch test scores, and good scores in the test involving the little two-wheel cart. In fact, puppies who had good scores in both of these almost never failed in training. Since then I have studied those who had good scores in these two tests but failed in training and have found that they had low scores in temperament. So, by watching these scores, we have a quite accurate system of eliminating poor candidates.

Four testers are assigned to teach heeling. They carry the puppy at eight weeks of age to the testing area, but heel it back to the kennel, as a puppy is almost always willing to go back to its litter mates. For the next four Thursdays they lead the puppy to the testing area and, after the tests, take it on a short walk where it will walk on crushed rock, concrete walk, and lawn, to adjust it to heeling and to different footing. On the fifth Thursday they lead it around the entire training area. Here it meets the cart coming toward it, finds the cart following and passing it, and meets the cart being rushed out of a blind alley in front of it. Eight score keepers mark the puppy's reaction as each sees it, four mark the good things they see and four mark the bad things. The puppy is led down a step, across a large piece of metal embedded in the concrete walk, up a step past an over-hanging projection, onto the crushed rock, and past a fire hydrant and a refuse can to a gate that blocks his way on the walk, where he meets a pedestrian. Every reaction of the puppy to these new experiences is recorded. He should get out of the way of the cart, but not panic. He should show that he notices the different types of footing. He should indicate in some way that he sees the overhang. He should find his way around the gate. He should show that he sees the pedestrian, but not be afraid of her.

In the other trainability tests the puppy is taught to sit by the tester, who places her left hand so that when she pushes forward it will bend his stifle and make him sit. Her right hand is placed on his chest to affect a jackknife arrangement. In all the training tests the commands, "Puppy, heel," "Puppy, sit," "Puppy, come," and "Puppy, fetch" are given just preceding the enforced or encouraged action. It is important to show the puppy what is meant by each word. Praise is generous at the end of each sit, come, or fetch. Come is first taught on the leash, no matter how willing the puppy is to come, to be sure that he will associate the necessity of coming with the command. By the third lesson the puppy is tried off lead and without the jackknife. Any time it fails to obey, the leash or the jackknife are again used. Each of the five Thursdays the puppy is given only three lessons in sit and come.

Fetch is taught entirely by play methods, except that the leash is used to direct the puppy to the tester the first and second week. The leash is also used if the puppy fails to bring the object directly to her. A rubber ball or tennis ball is used in teaching fetch. If the puppy simply goes to the object the first time it is considered satisfactory, but we have many puppies who pick the ball up the first time and come directly back with it. We also have pheasant and duck wings for the puppy who has no interest in a ball. Many shepherds as well as retrievers will bring a wing but will not pick up a ball.

We have come to the conclusion that what we are testing here is the puppy's willingness to do something for the tester. She praises the puppy profusely when it fetches, she never scolds or punishes the puppy if it does not. (Punishment for failure to retrieve is a common mistake made by obedience trainers.) We never say "Bad boy," or any other scolding word. We use only the word "No," which means stop whatever you are doing or are about to do. We never punish a puppy. This is more important in teaching fetch than in any other lesson, but it applies to all our teaching.

The desired result is to get the puppy to go merrily to the object, pick it up and bring it back to the tester's hand. The first week we give the puppy three chances to fetch after it has had a chance to smell the ball, see it bounce and roll, and gotten adjusted to the room. The tests start with the first command given; "Puppy, fetch." The second week the puppy has four chances, still on leash. The third week he is given five chances, starting off lead and reverting to the lead if it is necessary to get the puppy to come to the tester with the object. The fourth week the puppy has three chances. The fifth week the puppy has only three chances again. Any puppy who is not bringing the object to the tester off lead in the fifth week is rejected, for it will not make a Guide Dog. Usually such a rejected puppy can be taught to retrieve without much difficulty, but we have found that one who will not learn in the time allotted will not be a willing worker as a Guide Dog. This applies equally to all breeds that we have tested and trained.

The heeling testers score their own puppies and weigh them each week. Two scorekeepers score the sit, come, and fetch, and also give each puppy a grade on each in "Intelligent Response" and "Willing Temperament." In the last two, one scores the good and one the bad. Four testers measure the puppies each week. Like our other tests, these measurements include just about everything that can be measured on a puppy. The same group measures the grown dogs when they come back at one year of age for training.

This material can now be placed on IBM cards in metric system, and includes more than 1,500 dogs. From the first, a studbook register was kept and copies of pedigrees of all breeding stock. In recent years all the breeding stock not previously registered with the American Kennel Club has been registered, and pedigree books are kept up to date on all litters whelped. Only dogs of our breeding are now used in our training program, and the puppies are all raised in 4-H homes from the age of thirteen weeks until they are twelve months old. Thus, the entire testing, pedigree data, testing records, analysis, and the raising of the puppies from three to twelve months of age is done by volunteers who pay their own expenses, even to feeding and veterinarian care of the puppies.

The constant cooperation of Dr. Scott and his associates at the Roscoe B. Jackson Memorial Laboratory made it possible to develop our tests and evaluate them. As early as 1949, about two years after we started our tests, I had an opportunity to take what little we had accumulated back to Boston where I was judging obedience. Here I met Dr. Clarence Cook Little,* founding director of the Jackson Laboratory, and his assistant in his study of heredity on dogs, Miss Edna Du Buis. They went over the records I had brought with me. The records were very meager because, after the tests, it took another year or more before the puppy had grown and been trained; in a two-year period we had only a few complete records, and these were based on a passed-or-failed record as far as the trainers were concerned.

After looking over what I had to offer, Dr. Little asked me, "Have you planned any type of comparative chart which you can use to get a correlation between the scores given the puppies and the scores which the trainers give the same dogs in training?"

I explained that only recently had we received any information from the trainers, because the first dogs were only then being finished from the puppies we had tested less than two years before. The only information the trainers were giving us at that time was whether the puppies, when grown and trained, became Guide Dogs or failed in training. We were not being told why they failed or why they passed. However, I was able to tell him that the first year after the tests were used production showed an improvement which promised to be about two hundred per cent.

Dr. Little explained how important it was for us to set up a comparative record of how the trainers scored the puppies when grown. It should show all the things which we had scored while they were puppies, and how each individual's score in each category compared to the scores the testers had given. On my return we made up comparative sheets, went back to the beginnings of the puppies we had tested, and brought the records up to date. These records have been kept ever since. There was not the close cooperation between volunteers and staff at that time that there has been for many years now, and this made it a little more difficult to get all the information we needed. The trainers had one method of scoring, the testers another. There was some

* The results of Dr. Little's studies were published in his book, *The Inheritance of Coat Colors in Dogs,* Howell Book House Inc.

feeling on the part of the staff that the volunteers should stay out of the picture and, because we did not understand all the niceties of how volunteers and staff members can work together without getting into each other's hair, it took a little doing to get this part of the program working smoothly.

"So far as I know," Dr. Little told me, "this will be the first time that any practical breeding program has undertaken such an elaborate study of their puppies. So far as I know it will be the first time that a study will have been made of each individual dog's behavior so that it can be followed with a considerable degree of reliability from 'the cradle to the grave'. In laboratories like ours, our study of each individual is from one to two years. More important, your study bears directly upon what the dog is expected to do, and you give the dog ample opportunity to demonstrate whether he is able to do what you selected him to do. While your requirements are exceptionally high, this should make the finding even more valuable for scientific purposes.

"After having looked your tests over I have another suggestion that I feel is important. There seem to be too many puppies failing the tests. Your tests may be too difficult, you may be scoring the puppies too severely, or the puppies may be, as the tests indicate, not very well suited for your purpose. I suspect the latter is true and that you will have to find some much better way of breeding dogs than you have now. There are several ways to do this. You will have to find out, first, which of your breeding stock are producing the best puppies you are getting now. By using the comparative chart I have suggested you can arrive at a firm enough conclusion to direct you in the way you will need to go about your breeding program. You will be able to sort out which individuals possess genes which pair off well with other individuals, and thus produce the kind of puppies you need.

"Selective breeding is a slow process, but I think you will have to go through it anyway. By being alert and having accurate records of the results of each mating, and what it has produced in the way of Guide Dogs, you can avoid making the same breeding mistakes twice. What is more important, you can keep producing from the matings which give you good Guide Dogs,

95

and save some of the best puppies for breeding stock. These in turn, if properly mated, should produce better litters than their parents produced. As you find the relation between your tests and training record, this may lead you to understand your tests and their value well enough to actually pick your breeding stock by your test scores."

All this has come true. Today we select from the best litters from our best breeding stock the puppies with certain high test scores at twelve weeks of age for future studs and brood bitches.

"If you can learn to rely on your tests for your breeding you can save a year or two, because you will not have to wait until the litter has been trained to see what a breeding produced. In a program like this, the saving of a year is very important.

"Once you have found the good individuals in your breeding stock, I believe that you will want to develop your own strains. You will inbreed the dogs who carry the genes which produce the kind of dog you want. At Jackson Laboratory we have a great deal of experience with inbreeding, and will be willing to help you when you need us."

The inbred strains of mice at Jackson Laboratory, "Jaxon mice," are the most famous in the world. From one million to a million and a half of these are purchased annually by laboratories and scientists around the world because of their great value in experiments. Dr. Little, now retired, started these inbred strains when he was a sophomore at Harvard. Some strains here have never been bred to any except brother to sister, father to daughter, or mother to son in all the many generations since he started the experiment.

At Guide Dogs for the Blind, Inc., we needed a man who knew dogs and knew the Guide Dog work and how to serve the blind people better than anyone we had yet found. We also needed the kind of a stud dog that Dr. Little had suggested to start a dog dynasty for us.

After being fortunate enough to receive such sound and valuable advice from Dr. Little while on a judging assignment, it was too much to expect to find both the man and the dog at the same Boston show. This was exactly what happened, however. The last day of the show I was in the ring totaling my scores on the last dog I had judged, when my ring steward came to me and said there was a gentleman at the ringside who would like to speak to me for just a minute. This was William F. Johns, of whom I have spoken in previous chapters and who I had always hoped we would be able to get to head up our school.

We had dinner together and it was decided that he would come if I could sell the board of directors, many of whom were new on the board since the days when Mr. Johns had helped so much in getting our school started. This did not prove to be difficult, and soon Mr. Johns came to take over as Executive Director. When he came he brought Frank of Ledge Acres.

How important Frankie became at our kennel takes an entire chapter in this book. Our first awareness of his importance as a stud came when he sired from Britta v Modena Park our first one hundred per cent Guide Dog litter. About the same time he sired a very impressive litter from Guide Dogs' Olivia, a daughter of Orkos of Longworth UDT. From this litter we saved three for breeding. Odin is still a great force in our program, but we lost his two sisters after each whelped a litter. It was with Frankie that our inbreeding was started, and he proved an excellent choice.

Under the management of Mr. Johns, we coordinated the methods of scoring between the testers and the trainers. We defined what we meant and agreed upon 0 for failure, 1 and 2 for degrees of doubt, 3 and 4 for degrees of satisfactory, and 5 for perfection. The trainers agreed to give me a final report on all the dogs they trained so that we could use the comparative charts. New charts are being devised which can be used by the IBM punch card operator directly. At present we still transfer our records to an IBM transfer sheet. The following sheet is quite representative. It is easy for anyone to read. The second, or "Code Column," gives the scores as well as identification, ages, etc. Next comes the explanation. The IBM machine makes analysis accurate and easy.

IBM CODE—GUIDE DOGS FOR THE BLIND, INC.

Columns	Code	
1–3	1 4 5	Identification number
4	1	Sex (1) Male (2) Female
5	7	Ancestors selected by tests—number of
6–7	1 1	Breed
8	0	Weeks of age—pretest socialization
9	1	Home training None(0) Home(1) Class(2) Obed.(3) Hunt(4) Herd(5)
10–15	1 1 1 0 55	Date whelped, day, month, year
16–17	8 3	Weeks and days of age tested
18–20	0 4 2	Mating code (Number of litters of this breed)
21	1	Litter no. mating code (Litters by this mating)
22–23	0 7	Number in litter at birth
24–25	0 5	Number in litter tested
26–28	0 1 5	Number of weeks & days in kennel after test concluded
29	5	Number of tests given
30–31	2 9	Number of workouts given grown dog by trainers
32	5	Come—test score
33	4	Come—trainer's score
34	4	Sit—test score
35	5	Sit—trainer's score
36	5	Fetch—test score
37	5	Fetch—trainer's score
38	4	Heel—test score
39	5	Regularity—trainer's score
40	5	Closeness—test score
41	4	Closeness—trainer's score
42	5	Crossing—test score
43	4	Crossing—trainer's score
44	5	Traffic—test score
45	4	Traffic—trainer's score
46	5	Body sensitivity—test score
47	5	Body sensitivity—trainer's score
48	5	Ear sensitivity—test score
49	5	Ear sensitivity—trainer's score

Columns	Code				
50	3				Intelligent responses conditioned test
51	5				Intelligent responses unconditioned test
52	4				Intelligent responses conditioned trainer's
53	3				Willing temperament conditioned test
54	4				Willing temperament unconditioned test
55	3				Willing temperament conditioned trainer's
56–58	1	4	1		Age pup placed in home, weeks, days
59–62	1	1	1	7	Age dog entered training, months, days
63	1				Tests failed(0) passed(1)
64	1				Training failed(0) passed(1)
65	1				Home non 4-H(0) 4-H home(1)
66	–				Retained for breeding Stud(1) Brood Bitch(2)
67	–				Unusual sickness Ill(1) Died(2)
68	1				Unusual age trained Not(0) Yes(1)
69–70	–				Why failed training (see 11 reasons)

Note: This is quite representative of the comparative scores today. You can tell how well they correlate by comparing the test scores with the trainers' scores. All test scores are recorded at the time the puppy completes his tests, 12 weeks of age. The trainer has no way of knowing what scores the testers gave.

Hamilton Station, the Animal Behavior Laboratory at Bar Harbor, Maine, is one of the world's greatest. At this former show-livestock and poultry farm, dogs and other animals are being studied to find out why humans behave the way they do. Hamilton Station is the Behavior Department of the famous Roscoe B. Jackson Memorial Laboratory.

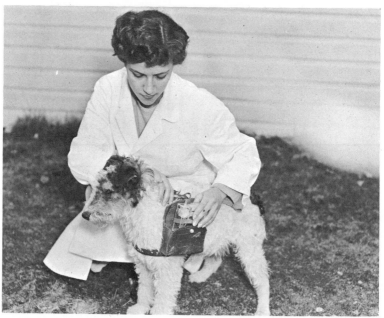

Years before Sputnik started beeping information to Russian scientists short wave radio told scientists at Hamilton Station how the emotions and heart beats of dogs were affected by new situations. This is part of the study in animal behavior.

100

CHAPTER VII

It Is What a Dog Does That Counts

After you cross the bridge at Trenton your way wends down the Beautiful Eden Road. The velvet green lawn meets the macadam on either side, and from the grass low shrubbery blends into the banks of maples and pointed firs. Then, through the gap in the forest, the unbelievable blue of Frenchman's Bay beckons. You turn in through a stone gateway and find long yellow barns under trees, edged by flowers and lawns, and there are great runs for dogs extending into the woods. You are at Hamilton Station, Roscoe B. Jackson Memorial Laboratory, on Mount Desert Island, Maine.

It was thus that I remembered my second trip to Bar Harbor in July, 1953. Juanita and I, with our three cocker spaniels, Peter, Rustle and Easter, had driven from San Francisco to spend the summer on the island. Juanita had never been on Mount Desert Island before, although she was born in Maine. She was unprepared for the dogs she saw in the runs, for at the time the puppies in the runs were mostly co-bascos, a combination of cocker spaniel and basenji. We will come back to them in another chapter, but the idea of breeding such dogs was such a shock to Juanita that she thought we had come to the wrong place for the right information about improving Guide Dogs. Actually, this very cross gave us some of our best information.

We parked our car under a beautiful maple tree and reported

to the office. I had come as a Guggenheim Fellow to work on my puppy tests with Dr. Scott and Dr. Fuller and the other staff members and summer investigators. Dr. Scott was away for a day or two, but he had left word for me to make myself at home and get acquainted with the program and especially with my fellow workers. These were professional specialists from many parts of the world who had come to learn from the experiments being conducted at Hamilton Station. Many had doctorates, some were professors, all were highly trained scientists.

In the seven years since I had visited Hamilton Station, many changes had taken place both at Roscoe B. Jackson Memorial Laboratory and at Guide Dogs for the Blind, Inc. The strides made in animal behavior studies at Hamilton Station had begun to attract a very serious group of scientists in this field as summer investigators. The atmosphere was something I had never before experienced. The freedom of thought and expression, the frank acceptance or challenge of any thesis proposed, the eagerness for facts, the total lack of the unreliable conversational rubbish so often heard among many of us who have never gone to the trouble to know definitely that what we expound as fact is entirely true—all this seemed too good to be true.

While I was becoming acquainted with my new associates, I went about with ears well bent so as not to miss a thing. I did not talk too much at first. There were several reasons. I could not believe that there weren't some prescribed thought controls, some limitations beyond which I was not supposed to go, some taboo over which I should not step. Where else could I have ever felt free to say exactly what I knew, or say I believed so-and-so because I had such-and-such proof that it was true?

So, a few days later, when Dr. Scott returned I asked him what rules affected a summer investigator like me. I said I enjoyed hearing everything discussed so freely and frankly, but I didn't know what I was allowed to say. I said that I had been asked many questions which I had refrained from answering until I understood his rules of conduct. I wanted to know his attitude.

Dr. Scott laughed, "You are certainly under no taboos here. Be just as frank as you wish both in answering questions and asking them. Challenge anything you cannot accept, but be prepared to make your point clear. We are doing a research study and such a study necessarily must be done without being prejudiced by any preconceived ideas. You will find that we not only dissect the ideas and findings of others to learn the truth, but we constantly study our own findings to see if by any chance we have failed to detect anything which would shed new light on our research."

And so at last I had found a favorable climate in which to study, with the help of the most competent men in my field, the hundreds of records I had shipped to Bar Harbor, a complete four-drawer steel filing cabinet full. Never have I found such unselfish helpfulness and understanding as I found here.

Dr. Terman and Dr. Stone at Stanford University had suggested that the studies we had made at San Rafael were of enough importance that the John Simon Guggenheim Memorial Foundation might consider giving me a fellowship to help me advance my study at Bar Harbor. Once they had suggested that I apply I found ten other important persons who offered to be my sponsors, too. So I had applied, first making sure that Dr. Scott would have room for me at Hamilton Station.

Dr. Terman had become interested in my work through Dora Perry, a mutual friend and a member of my Writers Workshop, who introduced us and arranged for extensive interviews with Dr. Terman and Dr. Stone. Their enthusiasm gave me the confidence to proceed.

We were fortunate to find a beautifully furnished, one hundred-year-old house at Sand Point, near Salsbury Cave, belonging to Mr. Irving Hamer. It had a lovely view of Frenchman's Bay and fine woods where the dogs and I could take delightful hikes. Three wine-glass elms shaded the front screened porch. The woods of maple, cedar and hackmatack swept along the drive, behind the old barn and carriage shed, the apple orchard, garden and berry patch to the woods which walled in the back of the property.

It was July 5th when we arrived, and the "Peabody" birds were mating. Never had I heard such a sweet melodious concert as they provided us for days. The air was full of their song. Then the mating season ended and the Peabodies settled down to

At seven weeks these two litters of Guide Dog puppies are delivered to 4-H children to raise as an experimental research project regarding two things, best age of transfer from mother to puppy raiser and whether line-bred litters can be relied upon as being uniform in character traits. These puppies were placed in weekly class training and given home training daily from the start. They attend class with older puppies. Bottom row left to right, 4-H members David Marcus, Joan Arruda, Ruth Stone, Martha Stone, and Kent Cooper, who are part of the Napa County Guide Dogs' obedience class conducted by Mr. and Mrs. Nathan Beauchamp. Second row left to right, Michael Varin, Richard Chivington, Gloria Gaunt, Shirley Gaunt, Timothy Strauch and Gordon Krook who are members of the Sacramento County Guide Dogs' obedience class conducted by Mr. and Mrs. Arthur Travis, Jr.

104

rearing their young, and quiet fell on the Hamer homestead.

The favorable climate at Hamilton Station and the delightful old homestead situated in so beautiful a setting made work on my research a great pleasure.

Shortly after we had gotten settled in our routine we had a visit from some of our dog-breeder friends. I got permission to show them through the laboratory. As Juanita and I took them into the headquarters building at Hamilton Station a pleasant, blue-eyed young man with black curly hair smiled a greeting and turned back to a desk heaped high with books and papers. He was J. Paul Scott, PhD., world renowned social psychologist and head of the animal behavior research program in which a million dollars is being invested in a search for new world knowledge to help mankind live more normal, better lives. Across the hall from his office three secretaries were busy recording the findings of the scientists on this great research staff.

A little ahead and to the left we took a peek through a one-way glass panel at one of the puppy nurseries. Each year in these nurseries, with their mothers to tend them, more than sixty puppies are reared. Scientists study the puppies in the nursery from birth to sixteen weeks of age to determine their natural behavior under various conditions. Visitors, of course, may not enter the nurseries, for what goes on in the nursery follows a rigid schedule. Varied and unusual experiences are avoided. Until recently, all puppies were raised in identical environments. Now study has progressed to where different environmental conditions may be prescribed for different litters.

Among the many things which Dr. Scott and his colleagues have learned in these nurseries is the fact that a puppy cannot be taught anything until he is twenty-one days of age. Then, suddenly, the puppy's nervous and mental capacities develop so rapidly that what he learns becomes fixed and influences his attitudes toward man and other animals throughout his life. The period from twenty-one to twenty-eight days of age is very important to the puppy, for this is when his faculties become very acute for the first time.

How sensitive a puppy is to his environment at this age was seen better minutes later, after we walked down the hall to the seminar room. Here, a young psychologist was sitting at the window with a pad of paper on his lap, recording what he saw in the yard. We stepped up near his window and took a look for ourselves.

There were three wire-haired fox terrier puppies at play in a fenced acre-field. Two played tag, running and barking in normal puppy fun. The third one, which we learned was a litter mate, stretched out on the grass, looked about him, spotted a five-gallon water pail. This he upset, then grasped pail in his teeth and whirled around and around until he fell from dizziness and the pail rolled down the hill away from him. When he could stagger to his feet again, he found the pail, put his front feet upon it and started rolling it about the field. He had not shown that he had noticed his brother and sister until they ran very near him. Now, he followed them out of curiosity, but when they noticed that he was following them, they chased him away. They would have nothing to do with him.

This lonesome puppy had had no surgery, no dope, had suffered no frightening experience which had set him aside from his litter mates. He was taken from his brother and sister when he was very young, only twenty days old, and raised isolated from all other dogs. He was carefully fed and watered and he even looked physically superior to his mates. His caretaker did not play with him or even talk to him. His playthings were the only things he had in his room, namely, his water bucket and food dish. At four months of age he had come in contact with other dogs for the first time in his conscious life. They were his litter mates but he did not appear to even recognize that they were dogs like himself. By this age he had lost his flexibility to social adjustment. His thirteen weeks of isolation from canine and human companionship, at this specific age, had molded his perspective in such a fashion that he would never be able to adjust to the society of either dogs or men.

At Hamilton Station the study of dogs by all these scientists is being carried on in an effort to understand why human beings behave the way they do. They are making a searching investigation into behavior with the hope that they can discover how we can raise our children, or at least our grandchildren, so they will not suffer from the maladjustments and mental ills so prevalent today. What happened in the life of this puppy, even at sixteen weeks of age, may well alert us to dangerous practices which are commonly followed by us, factors which seem unimportant because we tell ourselves, "The baby is too young to know the difference." We do this because we do not know about the critical periods in a child's life. Study of the critical periods in a puppy's life at Hamilton Station have opened up an entirely new approach to puppy raising and training, and have probably set up guideposts for child psychologists to use in charting their parallel study of the child.

While my work here was different from that of the other summer investigators, it was, nevertheless, a study of dogs to help people live a better life. What I came to learn was to be applied more directly. As I write this I have found it worth my while to cross the continent four times to work at Roscoe B. Jackson Memorial Laboratory, because I found there a great source of information about dogs and their relationship to man.

My personal study is concerned with the selection of puppies which have very special qualities, for the Guide Dog is given a responsibility in leading the blind safely under any and all conditions of traffic hazards, from any place to any other place that the blind person may wish to go, whether along a country lane, in heavy city traffic, into and out of heavily congested department stores, onto street cars, cable cars, or into trains, automobiles and airplanes. A guide for blind people must be so reliable that his master will experience the independence of a sighted person, freedom of motion and a life free from the apprehension of impending danger.

Many fine dogs who would be considered highly acceptable in any other field of activity can never properly qualify for the perfection of performance which we expect and demand of Guide Dogs at San Rafael.

An example of how much we have gained from this study is shown by the following: through selective breeding, the help of Hamilton Station, puppy tests in making our selections of breeding stock, and the evaluation of our dogs' genetic inheritances, nine of our litters raised between October 1, 1956 and October 1,

1957 were one hundred per cent litters; that is, every puppy in each litter which lived to maturity and was trained for a Guide Dog was a success. During the same period ninety-four per cent of all puppies bred from our selected stock, selected by puppy tests, when trained became Guide Dogs.

When we consider what we could have expected from our dogs had we not had this close relationship with Hamilton Station and had available for our practical use the purely scientific information so painstakingly assembled there, four trips across the continent to gain access to this knowledge seems a small price to pay.

We have been very fortunate in our foundation breeding stock. Because our school is strictly a private philanthropy, where no charge is ever made to a blind person for his dog, his equipment, his month's training at the school with his dog, and his room and board, and since the twenty members of the board of directors all give their time and talent without any financial compensation, dog breeders have been most generous. They have provided us with the best of their breeding stock without cost. From these fine dogs we have been able to select the dogs suited to Guide Dog work and thus improve our production records.

Mrs. Walter S. Heller, past president and board member, known affectionately as "Mrs. Guide Dogs," has visited all the best kennels in this country and most of the European countries for suitable foundation stock. The fine cooperation of dog breeders is evident by the fact that in fifteen years only two dogs and one stud fee have ever cost the school money.

Mr. William F. Johns, executive director, brought to the school the best dogs of a long line of German shepherds he had raised, donating them to the school when he joined our staff. One of these, Frank of Ledge Acres, has placed an impressive imprint on our breeding stock in the upgrading process.

Mrs. Heller and another prominent board member, the late Mr. James H. McFarland, made their best hunting stock available to us for breeding. From the Golden Retriever Club, through Mrs. Donovan D. Fischer, we have obtained top quality foundation stock. Thus, our retriever stock in the three breeds, Chesapeake, Labrador and golden have come from excellent obedience, hunting and field trial stock. It is our experience that dogs which do exceptionally well in hunting, in field trials, or make high scores in earning their U.D. in obedience trials, very likely possess the qualities we need in our Guide Dogs.

To get the best for any purpose it is necessary to start with the best available, and from them breed for the best to suit the needs for your own particular work. In order to select the best for your own use there is the matter of finding which will produce the best. We use two devices to determine what our breeding stock is capable of producing. Because every dog we raise has a chance to prove that he has what it takes to make a Guide Dog, the carefully kept records in training each dog show us not only if the dog was good enough to be a Guide Dog, but how good a Guide Dog he became. This is a very accurate production record which is rarely available to the private breeder. All of the puppies he raises are rarely, if ever, trained for the purpose for which the breed was developed.

The other device is our puppy tests, which show us, at twelve weeks of age, which puppies are best for our purpose. These tests are conducted once a week, beginning at the eighth week and running through the twelfth week of age.

Once you have found the best puppies there is still the matter of environment. Once you know the best environment to produce the best results, you will know just how the puppy should be raised from the time it concludes its tests until it becomes an adult. We have found that we get the maximum results by placing our puppies in the homes of 4-H Club members. Here they are raised as if they were the 4-H's members' own dogs, but have the additional advantage of working in a regular 4-H program under our own liaison representatives. Our liaison representatives are obedience trial people who volunteer their services to conduct weekly classes. They use our printed manual as a guide. These leaders help the 4-H members not only to give the puppies the finest care and home training, but to start them in obedience training classes at thirteen weeks of age. The manual they use was written so that the puppy raiser will know how to start the puppy in the kind of obedience training which he will need to know to become a Guide Dog. How these children serve

Guide Dogs in our studies is explained in other chapters.

"Can I, a practical dog breeder, use some or all of your methods to improve my working dogs? Can I hope to get more good dogs from my breeding if I follow your system?" we are asked frequently.

We feel sure that you could. We believe that several breeders or a membership of a local breed club could do a better job of testing and selecting in cooperation with each other than any one breeder can do alone. It would be better if the puppies were to be tested by someone other than the breeder. "Kennel blindness" should be carefully avoided.

"It is what the dog does that counts, not what he is," is an axiom at Hamilton Station. As practical breeders we might add also, "not who he is."

Even a great sire and a great dam may be completely mismated and produce inferior offspring.

At Guide Dogs for the Blind we accept this axiom as a truth: "It is what a dog does that counts, not what he is." And we believe that its acceptance is necessary for us to get maximum results.

There is a great deal more to this. If the new facts we have learned had not been established by such a reliable research program as that conducted at Hamilton Station, Roscoe B. Jackson Memorial Laboratory, we would be reluctant to believe many of the things which we now accept as facts. It is reassuring also to know that many things which we have always accepted as facts have been proven to be true. Today we have quite definite knowledge about how to breed better dogs, and how to raise them to enable them to achieve their highest potential. We know exactly when to do certain things to help them develop, and when not to do certain things which might make them as useless and as frustrated as that wire-haired terrier had become at four months of age—a dog who will be forever unadjusted.

Dr. J. P. Scott with puppies of the five breeds most used in his experiments found especially useful in studying the critical periods in the life of a puppy. The breeds here have inherited tendencies which pretty well parallel those of the human race as inherited in different families. The study at Bar Harbor is to learn about people rather than dogs. What we have learned about dogs from their study is a by-product. As different as is their inherited tendencies, all of these breeds when given proper socialization during the third and fourth critical periods reach satisfactory levels of behavior. These characteristics, which were found to separate one breed from another because they were so pronounced in all individuals of the breed, were: wire-hair fox terrier—born aggressive; cocker spaniel—born sociable; basenji—born wild and aloof; Shetland sheepdog—born with a need of security and approval; and beagle—born sociable but independent. All responded well to human direction.

CHAPTER VIII

When Failure Spells Success

At Hamilton Station one learns to take an entirely different attitude toward accomplishments. I had to school myself to be pleased when something I had assumed would result from an experiment did not so result—as pleased as if I had found my assumption to be correct. Research science is not set up to prove the researcher to be right, but to learn the truth.

Since childhood, Americans have been told, "You can accomplish anything you want to accomplish, if you go about it intelligently and work long enough and hard enough at accomplishing it." While this is a good incentive for achievement, there are some things in nature which are controlled by natural laws beyond which man cannot go. It is the discovery of these laws of nature which make research so rewarding. Through these discoveries the boundaries are set, the rules of the game are established. By knowing the rules the experimenter has accurate equipment with which to work and achieve.

It was through failure that Dr. Scott discovered the critical periods in the lives of puppies.

I feel sure that any of us who consider ourselves practical dog breeders would feel that our failure was catastrophic if we had worked for six years trying to teach puppies, hundreds of puppies, something, anything, and then to come suddenly to the realization that we could not teach them anything at all until a certain age, especially if that age was the first twenty-one days of their lives.

That was what happened to Dr. Scott.

It is little wonder, then, that Dr. Scott wore a very perplexed expression when he came out of one of the nurseries at Hamilton Station one morning and met John Fuller on his way to his office.

"I have arrived at the conclusion," Dr. Scott told Dr. Fuller, "that a puppy cannot learn anything until it is twenty-one days old."

Dr. Fuller is a most imperturbable scientist, but Dr. Scott's announcement stopped him in his tracks.

"I simply could not believe that anything could live to the age of three weeks without being affected in some way by its environment," Dr. Fuller told me later.

"I found it hard to believe myself," Dr. Scott says, "but no matter what I did with them, how hard I tried to teach them, nothing happened."

I first met Dr. Fuller in 1946. He was setting up his equipment at Hamilton Station to study the genetics of behavior as related to physiology. He had just come down from Orono, where he was professor of zoology at the University of Maine. His special field is searching out the relations of physical developments to emotional and intelligent developments. He is, like many of the men on this carefully selected team of scholars at Hamilton Station, a switch hitter and can play many positions in the field. He and Dr. Scott work hand in hand in their research.

Dr. Fuller at once offered to set up his own experiments to test Dr. Scott's conclusions and to see if there was some way a puppy could be taught something before it had reached its twenty-first day of age.

Here are some of the things upon which they agreed: the first time a puppy opens its eyes is anywhere from eleven to nineteen days of age, the average being the thirteenth. (There are records of puppies born with an eye open, or of opening an eye much earlier, but these are believed to be abnormal.)

The puppy seems to use the eye somewhat as soon as it is open, for the puppy starts to back away as soon as its eyes are

113

open. It is probably true that the puppy has to learn to use his eyes, because it will not wink unless the eye is actually touched. Moving objects do not cause the eye to close, nor does the eye follow the moving object.

There is no record of sound reaction before approximately twenty-one days of age; that is, the puppy is in no way startled by unusual sounds like a tin pan being dropped on a concrete floor. Its ears are sealed until then. At the twenty-first day the puppy may move away from a sudden sound, flatten on the floor or merely raise its ears. On the twenty-first day all sense organs seem to be functional and the puppy is no longer dependent on reflex responses to hunger, cold and touch. In place of reflex the puppy now has the ability to see, to hear and to smell, as well as to taste and feel.

There are also some interesting facts known about physical development which suggest that there might be some learning involved in this, especially in the way a puppy moves about, his motor abilities. Most puppies start to walk in an unsteady fashion on about the eighteenth day. There are records of puppies walking at twelve days of age. The change from the crawl to the wobbly walk is very abrupt, and the puppy does not return to the crawl once it has gotten up on all four feet. At this time the puppies start playing with one another by chewing on each other in the nest.

Up to now they have eliminated by reflex, from the stimulus of their mother licking their abdomens. Now they start eliminating independently and, at twenty-one days of age, they start leaving that part of the nest where they sleep and play to find another corner of the nest box where they can eliminate. (This natural, clean character trait of all puppies makes housebreaking reasonably simple if undertaken at an early age.) At twenty-one days of age a puppy is attracted by, and will go toward, objects which attract his attention through sight, hearing or smell. The tendency of the puppy to whine is much less. The several behaviors of the puppy before the twenty-first day, such as crawling, crawling backwards, swinging its head from side to side and similar neonatal behaviors, all disappear abruptly as soon as the puppy can walk, see, hear and smell.

At this age the puppies still dog-pile; that is, they huddle together to sleep. But they do not sleep as much as they did, and each puppy does some private investigation of his surroundings on his own when awake. They will leave the nest for a considerable time, but not go very far.

After Dr. Fuller had conducted extensive tests of his own he arrived at the same conclusion that Dr. Scott had, that a puppy cannot be taught anything until he is approximately twenty-one days of age. More recent study has shown that there may be a variation of some hours. It seems to be especially true that puppies who are carried the full sixty-three days, or even more, may acquire their sight, smell and hearing faculties a few hours sooner than those who are whelped before the sixty-third day. Dr. Fuller has also found that certain oft-repeated stimuli may indicate some learning can be attained earlier. (See letter at end of this chapter.)

Dr. Fuller's conclusions were that a puppy's memory span is too short for it to learn anything before it is twenty-one days of age. At most, he found that a puppy retains a memory of a previous stimulus for a few minutes, often only for a few seconds, before it is twenty-one days old.

I am sure we, as practical dog breeders, would have considered the experiment complete by this time, if not long before. But at Hamilton Station there is no stopping as long as there is any other known method of investigating the conclusion.

So Dr. Scott and Dr. Fuller decided upon two other approaches. Both had to do with the puppy's brain. What was going on in these puppies' brains? Was it possible that they were not physically capable of learning? Could they be as immature as all the tests indicated?

There were two ways to investigate this: one was by the use of the brainwave machine called the electroencephalograph. Miss Margaret Charles, a graduate student from the University of Maine, undertook this investigation.

The machine records the difference in brain waves under different conditions. In dogs, and in even slightly older puppies, it was known that a sudden sound, movement, or other type of stimulant, like the scent of food or the sight of a friend, would show a brain wave reaction on the graph made by this very sensitive machine. Reaction to sound is considered a good indication of awareness. This is called "startle reaction."

Miss Charles found that there was very little difference in the records on her graphs of the machine whether the puppies were asleep or awake, and none at all from a loud sound like a tin pan falling on a concrete floor. The newborn puppies showed practically no brain waves as measured by the electroencephalograph. At twenty-one days of age there was a profound change in the brain wave records, and in the differentiation between sleeping and awaking.

The results of these tests indicated that the puppy's brain is very immature at birth; at three weeks of age the puppy's brain starts to take on its adult form, and by seven weeks of age the puppy has an adult brain. This study revealed that the mature pattern of the brain waves of a puppy can first be recorded on an electroencephalograph at about seven weeks of age.

There remained one other method of studying the puppy's brain to determine the different stages of its physical development, an anatomical study of puppies' brains at different ages.

Dr. Scott asked Dr. Pinckney Harman, 2nd., professor of anatomy in the College of Medicine at the University of New York and associate scientist at the Roscoe B. Jackson Memorial Laboratory, to make such a study. The results of this investigation showed that anatomically the development of the brain paralleled the changes which Drs. Scott and Fuller and Miss Charles had discovered in the puppies' behavior. The growth, physically, mentally and emotionally, was uniform.

Dr. Harman has authorized me to quote from his report as follows:

> "Concerning the development of the dog's brain in the first three weeks of life, if we use myelination of central nervous system pathways as a criterion, as I believe we may, in a general way at least, we can say that a dog's brain is very immature at birth and that, although the first three weeks of postnatal life marks the development of a number of pathways associated with several of the cranial nerves, the brain still is in a relative immature state at the time that the ears open, which is in the neighborhood of 21 days of age. Thereafter much rapid development

116

takes place, so that by six weeks of age, as the time of social awareness seems to be dawning, most of the pathways of the central nervous system appear to be ready to function.

"It seems safe to say that the dog is insulated from its environment neurologically during the first three weeks of its life with the exception of a few of its cranial sensory systems (trigeminal and optic e.g.) and that conditioning of the dog as well as the establishment of complex behavior patterns would seem to be functions of systems which mature later than the third week of postnatal life."

To me, as a layman, Dr. Harman's carefully worded report means that the wires connecting the switch board in the puppy's brain are in the blueprint stage when he is born, and that it takes three weeks to get all the wires hooked up and the juice turned on, except for a few preliminary tests like the backing away, the wobbly walk, and the eventual wink. All is in order by the twenty-first day after birth, and connections can be made. By the time the puppy is seven weeks old, all minor problems have been ironed out and the circuits are in proven operational condition. Thus, this seems the ideal time for a new owner to take his puppy home. As will be seen later, this is especially true because from now to the sixteenth week of the puppy's life his basic character will be set by what he is taught. This will apply especially to his attitudes toward people and toward being willing to serve them the very best he can. The first twenty-one days of the puppy's life is when he most needs his mama and the food she can supply him, the massaging she will give him and the warmth of her body, and his litter mates. It is likely that the puppies need their mama until they are approximately seven weeks old, and the last two weeks on a part-time basis. If there is a time when they need her more than any other it is probably the fourth week, from the twenty-first to the twenty-eighth day. This is a time of very rapid development. The bud opens into a flower. For the first time the brain is sensitive to sight, smell and sound. The puppy becomes aware of his surroundings. His environment starts to shape his life. His intelligence and emotions begin functioning. To remove him from his mother for any great length of time during this week may be very bad for the puppy; to wean him during this week may upset him so emo-

117

tionally that he will never be able to compensate for the abrupt break. A week later, at twenty-eight days of age, he has already become so well adjusted that weaning will have much less effect. However, canine socialization is important if he is to grow up to be a well-adjusted dog. He needs to associate with his litter mates until he is seven weeks old, at least, and he needs some contact with his mother up to this age, if it is possible to give it to him. (Dr. Scott found puppies weaned before seven weeks were noisy and nervous. These seemed to become fixed conditions in the dog for life.) Dog mothers not only teach their puppies but also discipline them. This seems to be as important in puppies as it is in children.

At twenty-one days of age the puppy not only can start to learn, but will start whether he is taught or not. This change is so abrupt that whereas the puppy does not see (at least not very much) or smell or hear at all on his twentieth day of age, within twenty-four hours he does all of these quite well. Naturally he needs the security of his mother.

If a breeder knows that he will have to remove one or more puppies from litter around the third or fourth week and wean them, it is recommended that he do it just before the twenty-first day or after the twenty-eighth day. In the first case the substitute mother, who may be a person, must show the puppy a lot of special attention and affection during this period of awakening, and must continue to show it a lot of attention and affection at least through its seventh week. By the eighth week gentle discipline may be enforced, such as expecting the puppy to ask to be let out. This is of course the best time to make the transfer to a new owner, if this is what is to happen to the puppy. If the weaning of the puppy and its transfer to its new owner can be made at the same time, the research at Bar Harbor would indicate that maximum results can probably be attained. The new owner should take over, of course, and show the puppy every possible attention to adjust it properly.

This does not mean a lot of fussing, just common sense, good care, a few romps a day, and some preliminary training—a few minutes instruction a day in heel on leash and come to start with, adding fetch and later sit, down and stay. Housebreaking should be done at once. Many owners of seven-week-old puppies report that they seem to housebreak themselves if given a half a chance; that is, if they are noticed when they indicate their need to go out. Only mild restraints, except for the area where the puppy is supposed to stay, which should be quite definite at the beginning, are recommended at this age. From twelve weeks of age on, the puppy should be expected to mind every command.

This period of twenty-one to twenty-eight days is so strange to the puppy that at no other time in a puppy's life can he become so emotionally upset, nor could such an upset have such a lasting effect upon his social attitudes.

At the twenty-eighth day the learning stage has just become established, and the puppy is emotionally stabilized to where he can be taught simple things. What he learns during the next few weeks he will not forget. Like a child, he will learn things on his own if he is not taught, and what he learns may be things that he should not have learned; having been learned at this age, they will be very hard indeed to correct later.

One of the most important things at this time is the natural attachment a puppy of this age will make to the one who cares for him and instructs him. Many buyers wonder why the four- or five-month-old puppy they buy never seems to care much about them. The emotional side of the puppy goes along with his physical and mental development in a parallel course. By sixteen weeks of age all of these important developments are fixed in the way that they will continue through life. It is very difficult to gain the affection of an older puppy. Because the puppy needs someone to turn to for affection and guidance between four weeks and sixteen weeks of age, the person who finally substitutes for his mother in his life becomes very important to him and should take over as the puppy's mother gives up her duties, or, if convenient, make the transition gradual. In the time, at three weeks of age, when the learning stage began, to sixteen weeks of age, the character of a dog is formed. No matter how good his inherited character traits, if they are not given a chance of expression during this period he will never be as good a dog as he could have been. There is no way one can go back and make up to a dog in later life the things he failed to do for

119

him at this age. As we reveal more of the discoveries at Hamilton Station and Guide Dogs this will become more understandable.

By discovering he could not teach puppies anything before they were twenty-one days old, Dr. Scott revealed a basic fact about dogs which had not even been suspected through the thousands and thousands of years in which man and dog have lived together. This fabulous new concept has brought to light the critical periods in the life of a puppy. It is beyond doubt one of the most important discoveries man has ever made about dogs. All of us who are interested in dogs in any way are deeply indebted to him and his able staff for having pursued so relentlessly the facts, and for having made them available to all of us.

ROSCOE B. JACKSON MEMORIAL LABORATORY
HAMILTON STATION

P.O. BOX 847
BAR HARBOR, MAINE
January 25, 1960

Mr. Clarence J. Pfaffenberger
Guide Dogs for the Blind, Inc.
San Rafael, California

Dear Clarence:

In revising your book on puppy development you might do well to revise some of your statements about early learning in accordance with some of our latest findings, or at least to be a little more cautious about it.

John's (Dr. Fuller) original work still stands. As you know, he found that if he gave puppies ten trials on the formation of a conditioned reflex for electric shock no puppies indicated that they had learned anything before 18 to 20 days of age. Since then some of the Russian workers have done similar research. At 30 days of age they find that they obtain results within ten trials, which confirms John's results. At 15 days of age they find that they get positive results but only after 80 trials. They also found that using a different reflex, the reaction to food, they got results by 37 trials at 15 days of age.

This means that puppies younger than three weeks do show some sort of learning but only after very long repetition of training trials. We still do not know how permanent this learning may be. This (requirement of many repetitions) contrasts greatly with the behavior of older puppies and adults which frequently make an association after one experience.

Also, Dr. Stanley and Edna DuBuis have done some experiments with sucking which indicate that training does affect this behavior at a very early age although, again, after a large number of trials. The general conclusion would be that the very young puppy learns little if anything except from circumstances which are repeated over and over again, as in nursing, so that the general picture is pretty much as we pictured it before. Meanwhile, stating the conclusions in more defi-nite terms has had the good effect of stirring up people to do additional experiments with the young puppies.

Cordially yours,

JPS:jc   J. P. Scott

B. K. Miller photo

These two litters of puppies are typical of the first two critical periods in the lives of puppies. The German shepherds on the left are 20 days old. Tomorrow they will begin to live as in-dividuals, being alert to the world around them. Now they are like newly hatched chicks emerging from the egg. The yellow Labrador retrievers on the right will be 5 weeks of age tomorrow. They are on the verge of the first independence, that of aroused curiosity and an urge to investigate things near them. They will be about 12 weeks of age before they do much private investigation of far away places.

CHAPTER IX

Some Critical Periods in the Life of a Puppy

It is unlikely that any discovery made about dogs in recent times is quite as important to dog breeders and owners as that of the critical periods in the life of a puppy recently revealed through the research of Dr. John Paul Scott at Hamilton Station, Roscoe B. Jackson Memorial Laboratory, Bar Harbor, Maine.

Strangely enough, it was a lamb instead of a puppy that started Dr. Scott thinking about this.

"Several years ago," he says, "my wife and I rented a small Indiana farm, with six acres of pasture land which immediately began to grow up in weeds. Something had to be done and so we bought some sheep in the place of a mower. About the same time a neighbor gave us an orphan lamb which we raised on a bottle and kept in the house the first ten days of its life. Then we put it out in a shed in the same area with the other sheep. It went up to them once or twice but the mothers butted it away when it came near and it soon lost interest. We kept on feeding it and it became the most unsheep-like sheep. It never followed the flocks but grazed around the field in its own rhythm. Instead of being afraid of people it ran up to us whenever we came around. Three years later it was still fearless and independent of its own kind. We decided that Freud was certainly right about the importance of early experience, for a ten-day period of isolation had changed what appeared to be some of the most important characteristics of sheep, their natural timidity and lack of independence."

The above is quoted from *Children Magazine*, September-October issues, 1958. The article is entitled, "Animal and Human Children," by J. Paul Scott, Ph.D.

At Jackson Laboratory Dr. Scott and his associates studied hundreds of puppies as they grew up with their mothers and litter mates and were trained by human attendants. He has found the social development of puppies can be divided into definite periods based on the beginning and ending of certain important social relationships inherent in all breeds.

In Chapter VIII we explained how dependent a puppy is on its mother, or substitute mother, for the first twenty-one days of its life and why this is so. Some of us have worried because a mother will scarcely leave her litter, during the first five or six days after the puppies come, even to eat and to relieve herself. The puppy is so dependent upon her and its litter mates for warmth that it is necessary for it to snuggle up to its mother and brothers and sisters.

A temperature of eighty-five to ninety degrees is about right for the first week of a puppy's life. We have noticed that the puppies just seem to sleep and eat, and the mother constantly massages them with her tongue. This licking is necessary, not only to keep them clean, but to cause elimination, for the puppies at birth and for many days afterwards are not able to eliminate on their own. Nursing puppies eat a little and then rest against their mother's warm breast and she massages them. This is repeated many times a day.

The first critical period is approximately the first twenty days of a puppy's life. It averages about the first nineteen and a half days. There is a slight variation, which may be due to the length of time the bitch carries her puppies, for all bitches do not carry their puppies sixty-three days while a few carry them longer. Thus, some puppies may be more mature when born. For this reason a slight variation may occur in the length of the first critical period, but with all puppies of all breeds it is complete by the twenty-first day and is a sharp break. The critical part about the first twenty days is survival. Warmth, food, massage, and sleep are the things a puppy needs for this period.

While it has not yet been proved that the breaks from other critical periods to the succeeding periods are definitely as sharp as the break at the end of the first critical period, at Guide Dogs for the Blind we have come up with some data that indicates they are sharp.

At Bar Harbor, provided that socialization was started at the end of three weeks, no difference in the attitudes and attachments could be noted between the puppies who were raised in the puppy nursery and those who were raised in the acre fields. This added evidence that environment has no effect on the puppy until it is twenty-one days of age.

Beginning on the twenty-first day the puppy can see quite well, and can hear and smell. From now on, environment plays its part in the development of the dog. Suddenly the big world about him is opened up to his attention and he needs his mama very much. He can be handled, however, and socialization can start so that he will start to form attachments to human beings. For the next four weeks his brain and nervous system are developing, and at the end of seven weeks of age they have the capacity of an adult, but, of course, not the experience.

During these four weeks puppies socialize with their mother and litter mates and thus form their attachment to other dogs. This is the normal thing for them to do, and plays a very important place in the well-rounded development of a dog. If they are taken from their mother and litter mates before the end of the seven weeks, they miss some of their canine socialization and show less interest in dog activities than if they are left the full seven weeks. It has been our experience at Guide Dogs for the Blind that the puppy who does not complete his seven weeks of canine socialization is often the same dog that, when grown, picks fights with all the strange dogs he meets.

During the four weeks from twenty-one days to seven weeks of age playing, and even play fighting, begins. In some of the breeds this becomes quite serious fighting, and an order of dominance is begun.

For two reasons—(1) the puppy's need of socialization with

other dogs, which makes it desirable for the puppy to remain with its mother and litter mates until it is seven weeks old; and (2) the fact that a dominance order is developing which can have a lasting effect upon the individuals, making bullies of some dogs and underdogs of others—it is believed that the ideal time for the puppy to go to a new owner is at approximately seven weeks of age, which is also a good age for weaning it. The two things are probably best accomplished at the same time.

Dominance in a litter is an interesting thing to watch. At Bar Harbor it was found that if there are males in a litter the biggest male becomes the dominant one. If the litter is entirely female, it is not necessarily the biggest female but the one who talks the most. At San Rafael, besides the experience of having over-aggressiveness develop in dogs who did not remain under the mother's discipline long enough, we have had some bad effects from overlong canine socialization. I cannot remember a single dog who was raised with her mother to adulthood who could be successfully trained for a Guide Dog. Where two litter mates are raised together in the same home we have had the same results.

Puppies raised in homes where there are dogs not related to them have never been affected this way by the association with other dogs. This is a field which has not yet been sufficiently researched, but it certainly offers worthwhile, serious study. In the case of two litter mates raised together, one becomes a successful candidate for Guide Dog work and one fails, even if their aptitude tests were equal.

Experiments at Bar Harbor showed that when puppies were taken away from their mother and litter mates about the end of the fourth week of age and given a great deal of human attention they became very socialized to human beings, often forming such attachments to people that they did not care about other dogs. Some even expressed sexual desires toward human beings rather than dogs. Some were almost impossible to breed.

It is the natural thing, of course, for a dog to become socialized with its kind. It is believed that the fact that these individuals did not have this canine socialization with their own family continuously, until they were seven weeks of age, caused the unnatural results.

125

Socialization with human beings, by taking the puppy from the nest and giving it personal affection and some little training as early as five weeks of age, was found to be desirable. Thus, attachment to people is begun and the puppy begins to feel the importance of being an individual; this counterbalances its dominance experience with the litter, and it still learns to get along with other dogs. The frequency of the interval and the length of time devoted to each puppy during the socialization period may vary and still be effective. But regularity is probably very important. At Hamilton Station the puppies get regular attention six days a week at approximately the same time each day.

At Guide Dogs for the Blind, individual socialization is begun the sixth week. During his eighth week of age the puppy starts his tests. These give it a socialization period of about one half-hour once a week, and a close contact with a considerable number of people. Because the tests continue until the puppy is twelve weeks of age, we cannot place him in a home until after this time. Surprisingly, the weekly tests and individual attention the puppy gets once a week for half an hour seem to be very satisfactory socialization.

If a similar practice were followed consistently in any kennel, this might provide a longer period in which a puppy could be kept before being transferred to its new home, and substitute for the human socialization which it would get if it were taken by its new owner at seven weeks of age. I think this would be true if the kennel owner gave each puppy, individually, the same serious training in heel, come, sit and fetch as we give our puppies in our tests at least once a week, on the same day each week. This should be done out of the sight and hearing of its mother and litter mates. How we do this training will be explained later.

Our timing still fits quite closely into Dr. Scott's findings regarding the critical periods. We start socialization in the sixth week, and start our tests with training in the eighth week, continuing through the twelfth. Thus we intersperse some human socialization with the necessary canine socialization between the twenty-first and forty-ninth day of age. During the third critical period—from the forty-ninth to the eighty-fourth day—our puppies do not get daily socialization. They do get a heavy dose once a week, and they get about as wide a variety of experiences and instructions as their puppy minds and emotions are capable of absorbing. I think that it would be detrimental to give the puppies longer training and testing periods at this age, but it is possible that a daily fifteen-minute training and testing period would speed up their learning and possibly give more accurate data.

With our own, individually owned cocker spaniel puppies, we have found the daily training of fifteen-minute periods does speed up the learning greatly. I am not sure that more frequent testing is desirable. I believe that the nearer a breeder or puppy owner can stick to the ideal found in the Hamilton Station Tests, the better results he will get. These are summed up by Dr. Scott as follows:

"The evidence from puppies is that they have a short period early in life when positive social relationships are established with members of their kind and after which it becomes increasingly difficult or impossible to establish them. The same applies to their relationship with human companions. The period in puppies when we can best socialize them and begin their training is in the period of five weeks to twelve weeks of age."

Because man has developed many types of dogs with characteristics which apply more to one breed, or group of breeds, than to another, Dr. Scott selected a number of different breeds to make his study. He found a notable difference in test results in such breeds as beagles, cocker spaniels, basenjis, wire fox terriers, and Shetland sheepdogs. These dogs had been developed for hunting rabbits, birds, big game and rodents, respectively, and the last breed for herding.

While individuals in the breeds vary quite a bit, the difference found between breeds was very much greater, and fitted definite character patterns of the breeds. The most significant results were, however, that, as much as breeds vary, the critical periods apply equally to all breeds, and what happens during the critical periods is just as important to one breed as it is to another.

Since we now know that we cannot teach a puppy anything until it is about twenty-one days old, and that it is best to leave it with its mother and litter mates until it is seven weeks of age, the question arises, "When is the best time to start to teach a puppy?" The answer is, of course, as soon as it can learn, which is during the second critical period, twenty-one to forty-nine days of age. Like a child, a puppy is going to learn. If it does not learn what you want it to learn from you, it will form habits and learn from its litter mates and other associates things which may be contrary to what you want to teach it. The things which a puppy picks up on its own may be a block to its learning which will make success in training difficult or impossible later.

Concerning early teaching, Dr. Scott points out:

> "In considering the effect of time in relation to the commonly accepted theory that the past experiences of an animal determines in part his present behavior, it is possible to make three alternate assumptions: a) that the same experience any time in life will have the same effect; b) that the same experience will have greater effect earlier in development and in proportion to the youth of the subject; c) that there are certain critical periods in development (some of which occur early in life) during which the same experience may have a much more profound effect than at any other time."

Actually any dog owner would come up with the right answer and pick c) instead of a) or b). What we did not know was when the critical periods were, and how important they were. For a) we have the old saying, "You cannot teach an old dog new tricks." This old adage could well be re-worded to read, "An old dog, if he has never been taught anything, cannot begin to learn when he is old." For we are now finding out that a dog who has learned to learn when he was the right age can always be taught other things later. Most of us would have agreed that at one or two days of age you cannot teach a puppy but, like Dr. Scott, we would not have believed that a puppy under twenty-one days of age could not learn. This, of course, he and his colleagues have proven very effectively. That leaves all of us in agreement that there are certain times in a dog's life when it can learn best. Where we have been in disagreement is when these times are and how important they are. That is what Dr. Scott has cleared up for us.

The third critical period, from forty-nine to eighty-four days of age (i.e., seven to twelve weeks), he found to be the best time to form the man–dog relationships, and an attachment by the puppy which will permanently affect the attitude of the dog to human beings and his acceptance of direction and education. Considerable teaching can be done at this time, much as a child in the beginning grades learns things which are to become the foundation of his education.

During the second and third critical periods the puppy should have much individual attention to establish its self-importance as an individual. At this time it learns that it can be a co-worker with its human teammate. While training may be more or less in the form of games, the "pack instinct," which every dog inherits, may be cultivated by teaching it to work together with its master for the mutual good of both. The result is that the dog of its own accord yields to its human leader's control. Never again will the human partner be able to bind the puppy to him, or shape his character traits to follow the pattern which he wishes them to follow, as he can during the second and third critical period.

> "This is the natural period in development during which a puppy is unusually susceptible to environmental influences," Dr. Scott found, and then he concludes as follows:
>
> "The behavior patterns exhibited by dogs toward human beings are essentially the same as those exhibited toward dogs, and one set of relationships which can be set up between men and dogs is essentially the same as parent-offspring relationships in either species."

Scientists and naturalists have found that very young animals and birds often accept the one they know first as their parent. This varies with different species; that is, the age in which a period of complete dependency upon the foster parent exists may be from birth to twenty days, as in the case of puppies. There may be species in which it is even longer—the human being, for example.

Lorenz, in his experiment with greylag geese and jackdaws hatched away from any bird environment, found that both species preferred him to their own kind. Often they did not seem to even identify themselves with their own species. On a few

129

occasions, when they made exploratory flights with their own, they returned to him, rejecting the flocks for him.

I spoke of the study of dominance in a litter where the largest, strongest male dominated the litter, or the case of the all-female litter, in which the female who talks the most, growls and asserts herself, becomes top dog. In most breeds entire litters may be raised together. Even though there is a definite dominance order established, there is an adjustment where even the bottom dog gets enough to eat and a place to sleep.

At Hamilton Station they have never been able to raise more than three wire fox terriers together to adulthood. The dominance in their strain asserts itself in the fighting instinct, for which the breed was developed, to such a degree that the other puppy or puppies are starved by being kept away from food which is present at all times in the runs, forced to sleep outside the kennel on a cold night, or actually killed by their brothers and sisters. Almost any pup seems able to fend for itself against two, but none has been able to do so against three or more.

As an experiment, four wire fox terriers from a litter were isolated; that is, each had his own run until they were sixteen weeks of age. They were then all put into the same run. There was very little fighting among these, and none ever established a dominance over another. This adds to the evidence that, among litter mates of puppies, the dominance is established before they are sixteen weeks of age. There is an intense competition in a puppy litter for dominance between eleven and fifteen weeks of age.

Understanding the critical periods gives the dog breeder, as well as the individual dog buyer, an excellent tool with which to shape the character traits of individual puppies so that they may attain the highest potential in adaptability to the life they are to lead, and excel in the kind of work in which their owner wishes them to excel.

Up to seven weeks of age, a certain amount of trying-out dominance is good for a puppy. It causes him to have respect for other members of his species and it also develops in him something of an attachment to his kind. But to leave him in a kennel run with his litter mates until he is sixteen weeks of age without giving him special individual attention entirely away from his litter mates, including basic training and affection, is to deprive the puppy of very much of what he could have been. It may make him either a life-long bully or an underdog. It will certainly render him quite poor material for any training, and will limit his ability to adapt to human companionship.

From twelve to sixteen weeks of age is the fourth critical period in socialization. All critical periods do not run parallel; that is, physical development may parallel social ability, or it may vary from the period of socialization considerably. Most physical development and social adaptability do run hand in hand, but it cannot be counted on until you have the full information on each type of development, since they seem to be independent in developing. In this chapter we are treating only of things which have to do with social adaptability. However, the fourth period is one in which the two are quite parallel.

This is the age of cutting. At last the puppy, if allowed any freedom, cuts its mother's apron string and declares its independence. It wanders away from the nest alone or with a companion; it gets into mischief; it cuts its teeth both literally and figuratively. At this age it can still be socialized to human beings. It can be started in training. It will never make up, however, for anything lost through neglect in earlier training. This is the time when man and dog decide who is boss. Serious training can and should be started—a transition from play-training to disciplined behavior.

A puppy who has had no socialization before it is sixteen weeks of age has little chance of becoming the sort of dog that any one of us would want as a companion. Playing with the litter has some socializing effect, but it misses the important things: the development of the individual as a companion, and as an individual with self-confidence. There is nothing in socialization which develops a puppy to his highest potential faster than the simple expedient of taking him entirely away from the other dogs and having a pleasant session of just getting acquainted, or of fairly serious training.

At this age he needs to be free of distraction. If the trainer feels he needs to become accustomed to distraction, that can come once he is well trained and has complete self-confidence. There is no point in making it hard for a puppy to learn either how to obey, or to pay attention. The more ideal the surroundings, the better results will be possible. The puppy must come to feel that he is an important individual before the maximum results can be accomplished.

The time is so short—from twenty-one to one hundred and twelve days in all (thirteen weeks all together)—and once it is gone it can never be retrieved. The implications of what this short time means in the development of a dog are so great that it well behooves puppy raisers to employ this time wisely. It can never be made up at an older age. Dr. Scott puts it this way:

> "As different as are the inheritances of different breeds of dogs, all, when given proper socialization from three weeks of age to sixteen weeks of age, will reach a satisfactory level of behavior. Social relations are formed through the process of learning. They begin at a point where the first capacity for learning appears. It is important to remember that, while previous learning may be altered by subsequent learning, subsequent learning will never obliterate previous learning."

These beagles were raised in a one acre field with no human socialization until 12 weeks of age when they were given kindly socialization. When approached they cower, showing the wild pack instinct to stick together. Beagles normally like people and are easily socialized. These puppies have formed no attachment to human beings. At 12 weeks they will have a hard time to adjust enough to be acceptable as house dogs. Their lifetime attitudes are definitely fixed. Only maximum care and attention will make them even fairly acceptable. Each pup will have to be treated as an individual away from its litter-mates. It has not been allowed the dignity of being an individual. It has no ties with people.

CHAPTER X

Close as a Brother May Not Be Very Close

"Geneticists have found it convenient to develop their science from the study of easily observed characters regardless of their importance to the individual possessing the character. However, the significant genes of dog, mouse, or man are not those affecting the skin, color, or shape of the nose, but those which may influence his capacities for intellectual activity or the strength of his aggressive drives. Finding out how genes operate to control behavior is perhaps the most challenging problem of genetics today." Quoted from *Genes, Mice and Men*, published by Roscoe B. Jackson Memorial Laboratory.

Elsewhere in this same publication we read, "It is debatable whether primitive man adopted the dog as a domestic animal, or the dog adopted man. At any rate no other animal adjusts so readily to human society, nor does any other animal show the variety in personality which is such an outstanding feature of the dog."

In doing the research at Bar Harbor, Dr. Scott took advantage of the different personalities and character traits of different breeds of dogs to make his study of inheritance. His studies, and those of his associates, revealed that the centuries of selection by man of dogs for various uses have sorted out behavior patterns which are so fixed in inheritance that, while they make it easier for a dog to learn certain things which fit these patterns, they make it very difficult, sometimes almost impossible, for him to learn certain things which are contrary to his inherited pattern. (They also found that some breeds have a much larger range of learning ability than their specialized field has permitted them to perform.)

The groups into which dogs are generally divided for show purposes pretty well define the uses; most dogs in each group fit into the behavior pattern with the other breeds in the group. This is especially true of four groups: sporting, hound, working, and terrier, except that the difference between the sight hounds and the scent hounds is very marked between such breeds as the bloodhound and the greyhound.

(It must be remembered by the reader that this report has to do with two phases: one is the research at Hamilton Station, Bar Harbor, Maine, which is being done in search of solutions to some of the problems of mankind, and whatever the dog breeders gain from this program is a byproduct. The other phase is the research at Guide Dogs for the Blind, Inc., San Rafael, California, in which some of the findings at Bar Harbor have been applied in a practical dog breeding program. The applications of these findings have been carefully studied by the groups both at Bar Harbor and at San Rafael. I have taken much of the material from San Rafael back to Bar Harbor for analysis. Drs. Scott, Little, Fuller and Ginsburg, who have done much of the research at Bar Harbor, have all visited San Rafael. The San Rafael studies reported here have all been scientifically analyzed at Bar Harbor. The studies at both places continue, and there is evidence that there is very much more to be learned from the studies already made than the limited analysis reveals.)

At Bar Harbor, by using five breeds from the four groups mentioned above—dividing the hound group into two, one scent and the other sight—they found them to be ready-made tools for scientific investigation of hereditary differences in social behavior, learning ability, and emotional stability. The existence of such hereditary traits often has been assumed, and there has been a tendency to rely on a general impression that such was the case. There has never before been precise actual observation to establish the existence of these inheritances.

134

At Hamilton Station, during the first ten years devoted to the experiments in inheritance of the dog, more than four hundred puppies were reared from planned matings and each puppy given a set of tests which involved forty or more different measures of behavior in more than thirty situations. Tests began at birth and lasted approximately twelve months. They were given six days a week. Puppies were raised in identical surroundings to avoid environmental variational influences. (Where different environment was provided, such as isolation or complete freedom of the acre fields, these puppies were raised for experiments which had to do with socialization and environment rather than heredity. These experiments were very important to dog breeders, but they should not be confused with the experiments in heredity.)

To get the most use possible for the money allotted for dog feed, smaller breeds were selected from the groups. While the smaller dogs provided economy, it was felt that nothing was lost in their selection because each one used was well established; indeed, they were among the oldest breeds in the groups with well-established group characteristics. As an example: the cocker spaniels selected for the project were direct descendants of dogs such as Dual Champion Miller's Esquire C.D.X., grandson of Dual Champion My Own High Time. The basenjis were selected from dogs descended from recent African imports. Thus, the foundation stock represented as nearly as possible the ideal of each group. No new blood has been added in any of these breeds, to the best of my knowledge, so they have not been influenced by any changes which have occured in the breeds during the years the study has been under way.

The cocker spaniel has been used for more than four hundred years to search for game birds. In ancient times they were taught to sit quietly, or crouch, or lie down while the net was thrown over the birds they had found. Later the falcon was sent to strike down or capture. Today the sportsman shoots the game they flush, then, on command, they make the retrieve to hand.

The beagle, an excellent representative of the scent hound, has for centuries followed the trail of the rabbit, almost entirely independent of any control of the hunter. The contrast between the methods used in hunting the beagle and cocker over the centuries has brought about a natural selection for the character traits so positively that the beagle is today a natural "self hunter" who gives tongue in pursuit of game, following the game until it is captured, while the cocker spaniel is a silent hunter and, instead of pursuing the game when it is put to flight, "hups" (sits) until the game is shot and he is ordered to retrieve it.

It is true that a spaniel has to be taught to "hup," but that the natural instinct is there has been shown by the tests at Bar Harbor. This is the same instinct which make the pointers and setters readily trained to staunchly point their game and hold it for the hunter to approach to within shooting range—actually until the hunter himself flushes the game, in the case of the pointing breeds. Thus, the spaniels, setters, pointers and retrievers all work to the hunter and show caution when they approach game. They are readily trainable and the caution soon becomes a hup or a point, according to the training they receive. Thus we have a common character trait inherited by the entire sporting group.

On the other hand, the hound group, though distantly related to the sporting group, as written history reveals, is made up of two distinct sub-varieties: the hound that runs by scent, and the one that pursues his quarry by the use of his eyes almost exclusively. Both will run their game to earth without any guidance from the hunter. No matter what game is their specialty the hunter follows them, whether it is on foot, as with the beagles, on horseback, as with the fox hounds, or, if one waits with a little moonshine in the moonlight, until game is treed, as with the American coon hound. In every case the hunter follows the hound whose inherited character traits, plus a certain amount of training toward following only the variety of game he is supposed to hunt, make him a most able assistant.

The wire fox terrier was selected as a representative of the terrier group because it possesses the aggressiveness to deal with the type of game that a terrier is supposed to hunt. It also fitted well into the size desired.

A herding dog from the working group, which is small but has been consistently used for the purpose for which it was bred, is the Shetland sheepdog. This dog was selected to represent the herding dogs in the Bar Harbor experiment. The Shetland is very dependent upon the will of the shepherd, obeying every command, he is almost devoid of ability to make independent decisions. This character trait is very valuable for the type of work for which he is bred and, because he minds so well, he can often do more work and better than a number of humans could.

The basenji was selected as the dog to represent the fifth group both because it works like a sight hound and because it is so very different from any of the others. It is called the African barkless dog. It can bark, but rarely does. It has other vocalizations which are quite unlike those of any other dog. It is a pursuit dog. In African villages it runs in packs in the streets and is more a village property than a member of any human family. When it hunts with the natives while they beat the bush, it does not have to bark to chase the game from cover for the natives set up such a hullabaloo that the dogs can slip up on the frightened game and direct it into nets or out into the open to be shot without barking; indeed its silence, as in the case of the sporting group, is a decided asset for this type of hunting. Genetically it is the purest of any of the breeds selected, never having been cross bred with European dogs in Africa. Its general natural characteristics are aloofness, agility in action, and little or no inclination to form close attachments to human beings. (There is a lot of variation in different individuals, and it is the opinion of the researchers that a strain of basenjis who would form close attachments to their human families could be developed by careful selection in a breeding program set up for this purpose. Apparently their African owners had not valued this character trait and have never selected for it.)

The specimens studied at Bar Harbor are still so near the wild state that the females come in season but once a year, like the wild members of the canine family. It has been found that the cycle is influenced by the shortening hours of daylight. Thus, in Maine their season is always in autumn. An experiment, using artificially shortened daylight, was conducted by Dr. Fuller at Hamilton Station. By this means he was able to control the cycle and change it to other times of the year.

Pure-bred puppies from these five breeds were studied to discover what are the inherited characteristics of each breed and how they differ from those inherited by each other breed. Physical characteristics were studied to learn if these variations coincided with variations in character traits. (Appearance is no guide to behavior traits, it was learned.) Studies included temperatures, heart beats, muscle tension and respiration under various different situations, and the influence of different stimuli such as the presence of food, sounds, motion, and other animals, and the sight of familiar persons and other dogs.

Once the character traits of each breed were carefully catalogued by the records of the results of the series of tests, the question arose, how would the inheritance of one breed affect the inheritance of another breed if the two were cross bred? Would the result be the blending of the character traits of the two? Would one superimpose its traits on the other? Would a true Mendelian law control the results?

All tests, including such simple ones as placing a puppy on a scale to weigh it and leaving it there for exactly one minute, recording its behavior while attempting to teach it to sit quietly while on the scale, indicated that the cocker spaniel and the basenji inherited the most extremely different character traits of all the five breeds studied. In many cases these two breeds inherited exactly opposite character traits. In the test on the scales the cocker puppies soon learned to sit quietly (a character trait selected for cocker hunting strains for more than four hundred years). On the other hand, the basenji became increasingly restive under repetition of the test. It could be taught to stay, but as the lessons advanced it showed more and more the tendency to crouch in readiness to take off, and often enough did just that. (Sitting quietly is not one of the inherited traits of the basenji.) Most of the other inherited character traits were just as far apart as those exhibited in this simple test.

In conclusion, inherited character traits as shown by the various tests showed that, of the five breeds, the cocker spaniel is born liking people; he is born almost socialized to human beings. The three other breeds used showed various degrees of natural attachment to people, but the basenji tended to be aloof.

Dr. Scott calls attention to the fact that the dogs used in his experiments were in each breed from a comparatively closely related small group of individuals which were inbred with no introduction of genes from other dogs of their breeds, once the experiment was under way. This had two effects: 1) the selection of the same genes made the experimental puppies desirably alike for his purpose; 2) it more-or-less froze the type and character traits of each breed near the level the breed itself, and the individuals of each breed, had attained at the outset of the experiment. So, while many changes might be taking place in a breed in general circulation during a ten- or twenty-year experiment, those used in the experiment would still represent the breed and individuals as of the time the experiment started.

For this reason, what have been found to be typical breed characteristics of the particular dogs in the experiment may not now be so typically representative character traits of the breed in general, for breeders may have been selecting for other traits, or, in some instances, may have not been selecting at all for character traits, but for physical traits without regard for character. Naturally, this would lead to some variation. On the other hand, in such breeds as the basenji, aloofness may be being bred out in some selected strains.

This study, then, was not made for the purpose of analyzing breeds of dogs, but rather for the purpose of analyzing inherited traits. The original breeding stock selected for this experiment were especially suited for this study. The strain of cocker spaniels used was directly descended from the foundation hunting cocker spaniels which established the American cocker spaniel and had been used very successfully as hunters and in field trial as well as show dogs. They had the sociability and cooperativeness of that foundation stock. The basenjis, recently from the native dogs of Africa, had not yet been influenced by any concerted effort to change their natural characteristics, and were aloof and aggressive. (The term "aggressive," in a behavior laboratory, has no connotation of meanness. It means energetic and active, unrestrained.)

In using animal behavior to learn about human behavior it is held that any rule of inherited behavior traits which is found

139

Pure bred basenji (red) sire of Dog No. 3 from a litter uniform in color (black) out of dog No. 2, cocker spaniel (red and white).

Pure bred cocker spaniel (red and white) mother of dog No. 3. When bred to her son No. 3 (black) she whelped the litter brothers, Nos. 4, 5 and 6.

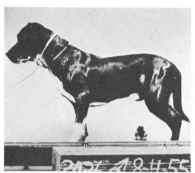

This dog is known in the experiments as a "Hybasco" (hybrid basenji-cocker spaniel). Red basenjis bred to cocker spaniels of any color always produced black dogs like this. Bred to his mother—dog No. 2, red and white cocker spaniel—he produced dogs Nos. 4, 5 and 6.

This dog was known as a "Cobasco" (hybrid Hybasco-cocker spaniel). He is ¾ cocker spaniel and ¼ basenji. He could do almost anything a cocker spaniel could do, but would not work well unless first trained.

A "Cobasco" litter brother of 4 and 6. He loved to train and work like a spaniel, but when he was praised he would freeze.

A "Cobasco" litter brother of 4 and 5. He looked like a cocker spaniel, but he behaved like a basenji.

140

to be true in a large number of different species of animals is probably relatively true of other species of animals, including man. Therefore animals of the same species as different in inheritance traits as the cocker spaniels and the basenjis studied, if cross bred, might give some clue as to what character traits to expect from human parents, one of whom inherited a social attitude toward others, a willingness to be patient, and a ready attachment to other human beings, while the other inherited an aloof nature and a restless and high-strung temperament.

With this in mind, a cross-breeding program was set up. Males from each breed were bred to females from the other breed, cocker spaniel males to basenji females and basenji males to cocker spaniel females. The offspring from these matings were bred together; that is, from the cocker male-basenji female mating; also those from the basenji male-cocker female mating. In the cross breeding, either way, the results were quite uniform no matter which combination was used, and all half breds were black.

In order to accumulate more identical genes of one parent than of the other, males from the cocker spaniel females were bred back to their own mothers, and males from the basenji females were bred back to their basenji mothers. This gave each puppy in the resulting litters theoretically three-fourths of its mother's genes. It also provided identical mother love and care for the three-quarter breds and the half breds from the same mother.

The photographs used with this chapter of six dogs in one family show the original male basenji and the original female cocker spaniel who, when bred together, although both were red and white, produced a litter of black with some white points, hybascos with flat coats. The basenji sire is shown in illustration No. 1, the cocker spaniel dam in illustration No. 2; a typical member of their litter who was bred to his mother is shown in illustration No. 3; the three extremes from the litter of six resulting from this son-mother mating are shown in illustrations Nos. 4–6: No. 4, a black-and-white smooth-coated dog; No. 5, a liver-and-white-pointed, smooth-coated dog; and No. 6, a black-and-white, medium long-coated dog. Their inherited

141

character traits were even more different than their appearances, and they did not in any way correlate with their appearances. The other three puppies in the litter varied somewhere between these three extremes, very mongrel in appearance. I had the privilege of using this entire litter for a training experiment which I will relate further on in the chapter. The laboratory dubbed this combination "co-bas-co," i.e., cocker- basenji-cocker. They were actually inbred on the cocker side, son to mother, three-fourths cocker spaniel and one-fourth basenji out-cross on the sire's.

Any field trial man who has ever seen a pack of basenjis running in an open field would be intrigued by the possibility of this breed combination. In the field the basenjis float along like the most graceful African antelope racing over the veldt. If a bird dog could be developed with this seemingly effortless action, and with the temperament and interest in bird hunting of a cocker spaniel, he would become the most spectacular field trial dog ever produced. It is well to look into how traits are inherited before launching into creating a new breed, however. To retain the desirable traits in an established breed is no mean job in itself. To combine the good traits of two such diverse breeds, eliminating the undesirable traits, would be an almost impossible task. Certainly it could not be accomplished in the lifetime of one man, if it could be accomplished at all.

How are character traits inherited?

There are different ways, depending upon what genes are involved. Some traits are controlled by dominant genes. Any dominant gene will assert itself in the offspring even though it is present in only one of the parents. Some traits come to the surface controlled by recessive genes, which must be present in each parent although they may not be evident in either individual. These genes have been inherited from ancestors, and have simply been covered up for a generation or longer. Most traits are modified by many genes influencing each other. There are even genes so antagonistic to each other that they are called "lethal." They can destroy one another and cause blindness and deafness, as found in some colors of dogs mated together.

There are also character traits which may be influenced or

controlled by a single gene inherited from one or the other parent. The influence of these single genes varies from absolutely dominant to only partially so. Some may be inherited only from males, others only from females.

I am not a geneticist. For me, the only way to get this clear is to paint a picture in my mind of what goes on. There are so many genes that they affect every detail of our beings. This is rather confusing, so let's start with the egg.

The egg is the means of passing on the inheritance which a bitch, or any female, has received from her parents. When it is fertilized by the sperm, there are combined the inheritance which the male received from his parents with the inheritance which the female received from her parents. No new genes are ever created in any individual, except by mutation. Mutations occur very rarely.

Every species has a certain number of chromosomes. Man has one number, birds have another, plants each have their own number. The chromosomes have been described as the very fine threads to which the genes are attached. Webster says, "gene— a factor or unit in the chromosome which is directly concerned with the transmission of hereditary characteristics."

Each parent inherits the number of chromosomes which it is natural for its species to have. If an offspring inherited all the chromosomes which each parent has it would then have double the number of chromosomes which it is natural for that species to have.

It is easy to see that this would be like the fellow who started to work for a penny a day and had his pay doubled every day. He soon broke the bank. Any organism can only inherit the number of chromosomes which are alotted to its species. This was true of its parents, grandparents, and all its ancestors. It is also just as true of character traits as it is of type of coat, of color, or of shape of body and legs. About the only thing that a breeder knows for sure when he mates two dogs, unless he knows what genes he is combining, is that he will get a dog. Two dogs will not produce any other kind of animal.

But if he knows the background of the parents he can predict a good many things. The relationship of the two individuals mated is always a factor, but, unless it is very close, it may not be nearly as important as a breeder may expect. Just look at the results of the mother-son mating in this chapter for evidence.

Tests are another factor. How both relationships in the breeding program and tests can help will be told in another chapter.

How does nature get out of the dilemma of pyramiding chromosomes? It goes about it very simply by halving the number of chromosomes transmitted by the sperm and halving the number of chromosomes transmitted by the egg. When the egg is fertilized the correct number of chromosomes is combined from both parents. The trick is that almost any half of the parent's chromosomes may be inherited, good or bad.

The way I picture this is: I draw two circles; in each circle there are all the genes which go to make up a dog, every detailed character trait and every physical trait; I cut each circle in half; I discard either half of each circle and put the two remaining halves together. That is one of the pups I will get from this mating. Unless I had some knowledge of what traits can be inherited by knowing the character traits of the parents and grandparents, I have no control over what that pup will be like. He is my dog for better or worse, and there is nothing I can do about it.

While every other puppy in the litter will get his genetic makeup much the same way, there is no guarantee that any two of them will inherit the same characteristics, unless both parents have some of the same genes. The more they have of the same genes, the more likely are the puppies in the litter to be uniform. If these genes are all good, then a uniformly good litter can be expected. While an excellent litter may result from parents who do not have the same genes, that is a chance result over which the breeder has little control, except by picking two good individuals who are quite similar. In many breeds today, certain excellent dogs of the breed have been used by so many breeders that a line has been established and any dogs from this line may get much the same results as closer breeding.

Here is a case of six inbred litter brothers, son-to-mother mating, that were three-fourths cocker spaniel and one-fourth basenji. They were given socialization, the tests and the training of Hamilton Station until they were twelve months of age. At that time I gave them both obedience training and field training. I am very familiar with typical cocker spaniel traits, having trained a considerable number of cockers both for obedience and for the field. I wanted to see to what extent these dogs had inherited true cocker traits. If some had inherited cocker traits, I wanted to know which of them had so inherited. In their cocker spaniel ancestry they had some of the great ancestors in both types of performances.

I first gave them time to adjust to me. Each day I took each one at a different time to my office and gave it the run of the place. I gave it much praise and encouragement. I have worked with thousands of dogs and never before found such indifferent attitudes. None ever showed that it had become very attached to me. All the pure-bred cockers at Bar Harbor showed a great desire to be friendly and to cooperate.

One of them did adopt me; that is, he did not want any of the others to have anything to do with me. The days on which I took him out of the run first for his grooming and training suited him fine. He could learn most of the things that I could teach a cocker spaniel. On those days he was an excellent pupil. But if I took another puppy out before him, he was sure to act up. The more puppies I took before him the more he acted up. If he was left until the last he was almost uncontrollable, showing great agitation.

Another was a miserable specimen in conformation, but he loved to learn. He was a good retriever and he would heel close like a shetland sheepdog. But praise embarrassed him. If I praised him he would freeze in whatever posture he was.

The third one, although he looked like a fine cocker spaniel, was not interested in retrieving, not even a pheasant wing. He froze when petted or praised. He could not have been less like a cocker spaniel in temperament.

The behavior of the other three was divided; one was much like the first and looked a good deal like him. The other two were bitches and showed some spaniel, but of an inferior quality physically, and were much like the third one in behavior.

My conclusion is: character traits are inherited; the manner in which they are inherited is known; there are breeding methods

When Mr. Johns became Executive Director of Guide Dogs for the Blind, Inc., he brought with him several dogs which he considered most suitable for breeding ideal Guide Dogs. One of them was Frank of Ledge Acres whom he had raised. He bred Frankie to all the best shepherd bitches, including his daughters, at San Rafael. The results were remarkable, especially from Frankie's daughters and granddaughters. Today three German shepherd strains are being created at Guide Dogs: No. 1—more than half Frankie; No. 2—half Frankie; and No. 3 has as much Orkos of Longworth as we can still salvage along with Frankie. If any of these strains start to show weakness because of too close breeding we can go out to one of the others without changing type. In fact, outcrosses between the strains will be planned to keep up vitality.

which will produce to a large degree the traits desired by the breeder; but a dog's appearance has nothing to do with the way he will behave.

"Each breed has a number of traits of behavior and temperament that combine to make a dog which is highly trainable for the breed's purpose," Dr. Scott says. "These traits include such things as aggressiveness, interest in food, quickness to form habits, etc.

"What is desirable in one breed may be bad in another. These traits are inherited independently of each other, which is the reason that it is so difficult to breed an ideal dog of a fine type. A very poor performer may have only one trait missing, but this throws off the entire combination. At the same time the very difficulty of the goal is one of the things which makes dog breeding such a fascinating occupation and so rewarding when success is achieved with a great individual or better still with a great dominant strain."

I have been fortunate to have Dr. Benson Ginsburg, world-renowned geneticist, to help me in analyzing the genetic effect obtained in our German shepherd breeding program. From this analysis we got some wonderful surprises. They point the way to better Guide Dogs. They confirm that our breeding plan has been sound, but show us how to greatly improve upon it. A later chapter in this book will be devoted to the study and the results.

CHAPTER XI

To Have, to Hold, and to Improve

No matter what our goal is in a breeding program, it is imperative that we start with individual specimens as near our ideal as it is possible for us to obtain. The big problem in breeding is to hold these ideal characteristics and improve upon them.

At Guide Dogs for the Blind, we have been able to hold the traits we desired from our foundation stock and to improve upon them by carefully selecting the offspring of our foundation breeding stock through the use of the puppy test scores in two tests, "fetch" and the "eye tests," both of which have been explained in previous chapters.

By having ascertained that these two tests are excellent predictors for selecting the puppies from each litter that will make successful Guide Dogs, and that these character traits are definitely inherited, we have been able to select our studs and brood bitches at twelve weeks of age with confidence, a confidence which has been justified by the results obtained in the litters they themselves produce. This has greatly accelerated our rate of improvement, saving us at least one year at the outset, and pyramiding this as the program progresses.

What makes this possible and how it works has been a subject studied by me with the aid of some of America's most eminent scientists during the last five years. What we have learned seems to be significant, and some of it is probably entirely new to the science of dog breeding as practiced anywhere.

This litter has an inbred coefficient of 0.48, which is among the highest ever reported in dogs. All are well formed and have no physical or temperamental faults. All have passed their puppy tests with above average scores. They were X-rayed at four weeks and have above average hip and pelvic assembly; two are almost perfect. Bottom row left, Emmabelle Herak holding three of the litter; right, Fay Harwood holding the other three. Top row left, Mr. Fred Maynard, assistant to Mr. Pfaffenberger, holding Guide Dogs' Fancy, dam; right, Dr. Benson Ginsburg holding Guide Dogs' Denny, sire. Age of the puppies when picture was taken was 12 weeks.

As in most studies of this kind, there has been a succession of discoveries which had led us on and on. While analyzing our tests (which had accumulated up to June, 1953) for correlation of the testers' and the trainers' scores, I was being helped and directed by Dr. J. Paul Scott and Dr. John L. Fuller. One day, while helping me, Dr. Fuller asked, "Have you noticed how many of the puppies that have passed your fetch test have become Guide Dogs?"

Up to this time I had not thought of selecting one test as a predictor, having my mind set on getting all the tests to function in the way I had hoped they would and in trying to find out, if they did not, why they did not.

A little further study of our data revealed that the fetch test was indeed quite an accurate predictor for the selection of the puppies that were potential Guide Dogs. When we combined these results with those of the eye tests, the two together became very reliable predictors.

Dr. Scott was equally impressed with our discovery, and suggested ways of finding out how we were getting our good fetch scores, that is, were they inherited? I had just started on this search when Dr. Little dropped into my office with two members of the Scientific Advisory Board. When I told them what we had discovered and what I was trying to do, they were all very much interested. Dr. Little said, "I am sure that you will find that your fetch character trait is inherited. What you need to know is how it is inherited. It may be by a single gene. It may be by a simple Mendelian pattern. It may come from just one sex, sire or dam. Once you know how it is inherited you should be able to greatly improve your breeding program. Your specimens should be better and your litters should be uniform and dependable. I believe you have come up with a valuable discovery and recommend that you follow it through until you have determined how this trait is inherited. It can be done."

Among the things recommended by Dr. Little were the mating of dogs chosen for their high fetch scores and a study of the resulting litters. He also recommended a study of the puppies we had already produced that had this desirable quality, and an analysis of their ancestry to see if some common ancestor was

150

contributing heavily to produce these desired results, and line-breeding of the descendants of such producers, going back to the original stock if possible.

Advice of this kind by Dr. Clarence Cook Little is not to be taken lightly. He is "the man who made the mouse a respected citizen." His strains of line-bred and in-bred mice have made possible uniform inquiry into the origin, causes and treatment of many of the non-communicable diseases such as cancer, leukemia, and diabetes in great medical research centers throughout the world. Because of their homozygosity, millions of the Jackson laboratory mice have been purchased by research laboratories in all parts of the world.

While it is true that what Dr. Little has done with the Jackson mice no dog breeder would want to do, or ever could do in a lifetime, what he has done points a way toward holding what one has in one's foundation stock, and also discredits the bugaboo so generally feared by dog-breeders concerning the deteriorating results which will come from close line-breeding. Some strains of Dr. Little's mice have never been bred out of the family at all for nearly fifty years, having been the results of brother to sister, mother to son, and father to daughter, mating every generation. At least one strain has been bred litter brother to litter sister, generation after generation, for more than two hundred and fifty generations with no exceptions. All this strain is now just about as identical as identical twins. This is what makes them so useful for experimental work. In all parts of the world the scientists are studying the same mouse, but in many thousands of individuals. At this time it seems unlikely that there ever will be a dog that would represent our ideal so perfectly that we would want to set his genes in such a fixed pattern that it would be very difficult to successfully introduce genes from a new strain at will.

There are two ways to use pedigrees to evaluate the relationship of an ancestor to its progeny. As explained in Chapter X, each puppy gets half of its chromosomes from each parent and, thus, half its genes, but never do two puppies that are not identical twins get exactly identical genes from their parents, even though they are litter mates.

151

As any breeder knows, the litter mates of an outstanding dog are unfortunately not carbon copies of this dog. When an unusually good dog shows up, the problem for the breeder becomes one of getting as many of the good characteristics of this dog into as many of his get as possible. Although many dog breeders shy away from the mating of close relatives, cattle breeders have used line-breeding of daughters and granddaughters to an outstanding sire with great effectiveness in order to intensify the genetic relationship of the progeny to this sire and thereby increase both (a) the resemblance of the progeny to him and to each other, and (b) the likelihood of maintaining the favorable characteristics in their stock for generations to come. Line-breeding of this type is a form of inbreeding. Inbreeding consists simply of the mating of relatives. Inbreeding increases the likelihood that an individual will inherit the same genes from each parent. Geneticists measure inbreeding mathematically by the use of a scale going from 0 to 1 (or 100%). On this scale, 0 means that there has been no increase in the proportions of like genes inherited from common ancestors, and 1 (or 100%) means that each individual is a genetic carbon copy of every other one. An inbreeding coefficient of 1 is not practically feasible with dogs. It would take minimally thirty generations of brother x sister matings to approximate it, even assuming that no undesirable hidden (recessive) traits would show up to interfere with the inbreeding program. If a non-inbred dog could be both the sire and dam of its own offspring, the litter would have an inbreeding coefficient of only 0.5.

Note that inbreeding by itself simply increases the proportion of identical genes coming from both the sire and the dam. It does this at random and is, therefore, as likely to fix undesirable genes in the population as desirable ones. Line-breeding is a form of inbreeding that attempts to be selective about the genes that are to become fixed in the progeny by increasing the genetic relationship to the most outstanding individuals in the pedigree, thereby increasing the resemblance of future generations to these individuals and also insuring a higher probability that these individuals, when selectively bred to each other, will continue to show the desirable combinations of traits that will characterize this line. The use of the inbreeding coefficient to monitor the increase in genetic uniformity, together with the practice of selective line-breeding in which the undesirable genetic combinations are discarded and the superior ones intensified and retained, constitute two ways of utilizing pedigrees to improve stock.

In 1948 Mr. Johns inbred some of our best stock, whose only fault was that they were show-size shepherds; this is too large for Guide Dogs. The object of the inbreeding was to retain quality and reduce size. We had no "fetch" puppy test scores on Frankie, our foundation sire, but we did on the half sisters used in the experiment and on their mother. They were as follows, with a short pedigree showing the relation of each dam to the other:

Orkos of Longworth, UDT

Guide Dogs' Olivia (Fetch 4)

Guide Dogs' Doris (Fetch 5)

Orkos of Longworth

Guide Dogs' O'Henry (Fetch 3)

Guide Dogs' Doris (Fetch 5)

and her half-sister

Guide Dogs' Hula (Fetch 4)

Balko of Rocky Reach, CD

Guide Dogs' Doris (Fetch 5)

Quip of San Miguel

From Frankie and Olivia we kept Odin, and from Frankie and Hula we kept Gretchen. When bred together we got a hundred per cent Guide Dog litter. A chart showing a study of the results, and explanations of some of the conclusions are included in this chapter.

Up until 1953 it had not been known to us that "fetch" was such an important predictor, and we had not thought of the

153

COMPARATIVE CHART OF TESTING AND TRAINING
GERMAN SHEPHERD ODIN x GRETCHEN LITTER

1. Actual Puppy Test Scores
2. Actual Trainers' Scores

		Predicted Success Scores Based on Parents' Puppy Tests			Litter					
		Sire	Dam							
Name		Odin	Gretchen	Expectancy	Nicky	Nemo	Nina	Nadine	Nelda	Nada
Wright's Inbreeding Coefficient		.0010	.0015		.1883	.1883	.1883	.1883	.1883	.1883
Sex		male	female		male	male	female	female	female	female
Number Puppy Tests		5	5		5	5	5	5	5	5
Number Adult Training Workouts		5	5		22	28	28	22	29	27
Come	Puppy Tests 1	3	4	3.5	2	5	4	4	4	5
	Adult Train. 2				2	4	4	3	3	3
Sit	Puppy Tests 1	4	2	3	3	5	4	4	3	5
	Adult Train. 2				3	4	4	3	3	4
Fetch	Puppy Tests 1	3	4	3.5	2	4	4	3	3	2
	Adult Train. 2				3	4	4	3	3	4
Traffic Check	Puppy Tests 1	4	4	4	5	3	5	5	4	2
	Adult Train. 2				3	4	2	2	1	2
Crossings	Puppy Tests 1	4	3	3.5	5	5	5	5	5	5
	Adult Train. 2				3	4	3	4	4	4
Closeness	Puppy Tests 1	4	4	4	5	5	5	5	5	4
	Adult Train. 2				3	4	4	3	4	3
Body Sensitivity	Puppy Tests 1	4	5	4.5	5	5	5	5	5	5
	Adult Train. 2				5	4	5	5	5	5
Ear Sensitivity	Puppy Tests 1	4	5	4.5	4	5	4	5	5	5
	Adult Train. 2				5	4	4	5	5	5
Intelligent Response to New Experience	Puppy Tests 1	4	5	4.5	4	4	4	4	4	5
Intelligent Response to Guide Dog Training	Adult Train. 2				2	4	4	3	4	3
Willing	Puppy Tests 1	4	5	4.5	5	4	5	5	4	5
Temperament	Adult Train. 2				3	4	4	3	4	3
Age sent to home		15 wk.	17 wk.		14 wk.	14 wk.	14 wk.	14 wk.	14 wk.	14 wk.
Age trained		not	not		47 wk.	47 wk.	43 wk.	43 wk.	43 wk.	43 wk.
Passed Puppy Tests		yes	yes		yes	yes	yes	yes	yes	yes
Passed Training		yes	yes		yes	yes	yes	yes	yes	yes
Pelvic X Ray Evaluation		5	4	4.5	3	3	3	2	3	3
Adult Height – Centimeters*		54.0	55.8	54.9	55.6	56.9	53.5	54.8	51.2	52.3
Adult Weight – Kilograms*		33.2	34.4	33.8	25.3	31.0	24.2	25.0	24.2	27.5

*Age of measurement and weight: Odin – 60 weeks; Gretchen – 120 weeks; Litter – same as "age trained"

154

necessity of selecting our breeding stock by giving such close attention to the results of the fetch test and the eye tests. Having made this discovery we started to select the puppies that made the highest scores in these two tests for studs and brood bitches and breeding them together. Two things happened. One was that we found that most of our high-score puppies came from two combinations: Frank of Ledge Acres bred to Britta of Modena Park, an Austrian import; and from Frankie when bred to the two sisters in the above pedigree, Olivia and Hula. This justified Mr. John's faith in Frankie as a Guide Dog producer, and it also brought about a rather closely line-bred strain, which is now known as the Frankie Strain. The offspring that produced the best most consistently proved to be those that were bred in line.

An illustrative litter resulting from a line-breeding to Frankie is shown in the chart page. In this case the sire (Odin) and dam (Gretchen) of the litter were both sired by Frankie out of closely related bitches resulting in a one hundred-and-fifty-fold increase in the in-breeding coefficient of the litter over that of the sire and dam. Of the ten puppy tests represented in the chart, the average score for the litter of six was as high as that of the highest scoring parent on five tests; higher than that of either parent on three tests; equal to the average score of the parents on one test; and equal to the lowest scoring parent on one test. Thus, in nine out of the ten tests, there was improvement over the lower scoring parent, and in eight of the ten tests the puppies scored as well or better than the higher-scoring parent. Since the higher-scoring parent had a perfect score in four tests, the field for improvement was restricted, and the litter had a remarkable record indeed! All were put into Guide Dog training and all became successful guides.

The pelvic x-rays of the parents were better than those of their get. However, none of the puppies showed subluxation.

Since the adult heights and weights represented on the chart were taken at different ages for sire, dam and litter, no meaningful comparisons can be made with respect to weights. The heights stabilize earlier, so that it is instructive to point out that the average for the litter is within 0.8 centimeters of that of the parents, and the total variation, taking each sex separately, is 3.6 centimeters, or about an inch and a half.

What this line-breeding has achieved is uniformity of offspring at a level equal to, or better than, the good qualities of each parent.

In 1957, when I returned to Hamilton Station and discussed this with Dr. Scott and Dr. Fuller, we decided that it would be well at this time to analyze the results of both line-breeding and of breeding from the fetch character trait. With Dr. Fuller's help I set up a form upon which every German shepherd puppy we had *raised* and *tested* would be shown with his fetch score, together with his sire and dam and their fetch scores if they, too, had been puppy tested. This involved seven hundred and twelve puppies and their parents, and took three sheets of drawing board-sized graph paper to tabulate results, plus pedigrees, for each breeding to show relationships greater than parent.

Frankly, when I tried to analyze this at home in California I got in over my head. Fortunately for me, Dr. Scott happened to be visiting at Guide Dogs at the time, and while we were discussing our problems with Dr. Benson Ginsburg, Professor of Biology at the University of Chicago and Scientific Associate at the Roscoe B. Jackson Memorial Laboratory, Dr. Ginsburg offered to help me out of my dilemma. He is a ranking geneticist with a long-standing interest in dog heredity and an interest in my studies since we worked together at Bar Harbor in 1953–54. At the time he was a Fellow at the Center for Advanced Study in the Behavioral Sciences, on the Stanford University campus, a Ford Foundation project to pool and improve man's knowledge of behavior, Dr. Ginsburg offered, and Dr. Scott heartily agreed, to have the scientific analysis done at Stanford by experts at the center under Dr. Ginsburg's direction. Dr. Ginsburg has become so intrigued with what we are finding out that he has done nearly all the analysis personally. He has authorized this statement:

"I consider this one of the five or six significant projects on dog genetics and behavior. Three of those known to me are academic: Hamilton Station under Drs. Scott and Fuller; Cornell under Dr. Stockard; and my own Chicago project. Of the more utilitarian projects in terms of both practical development and theoretical information, there was Fortunate Fields, reported in 1934 by Humphrey and Warner, resulting in a superior European strain of German Shepherds (Orkos of Longworth was descended from this strain); the development of the Boveagh strain of Border Collies by Dr. Kelley in Australia; the development of the Dog of Canaan by the Mencls in Israel; and the development of the Frankie Strain at San Rafael by Guide Dogs for the Blind, Inc.

"Fortunate Fields had no dogma and set no theoretical limit on in-breeding. (The amount that can be tolerated will vary with the stock, depending upon the number of deleterious recessive genes, bad genes which are carried, but not shown, transmitted by the foundation animals.) It is not informative to compare coefficients of in-breeding between two lines unless the one doing the analysis knows the amount of homozygosity there was in the foundation stock. Homozygous genes are genes in which the contribution made by both parents are identical. The in-breeding coefficient merely measures the average increase in homozygosity. Thus, a coefficient of 20% might mean a very different total according to the amount of homozygosity that existed in the foundation stock when the line or strain was started.

"In his Boveagh Strain Kelley found no deleterious effects with an in-breeding coefficiency of 20%. The Canaan Dog is derived from the native Pariah dogs of the Middle East to produce a breed suitable for arduous work in the desert.

"At Guide Dogs for the Blind, Inc., the Frankie Strain has a 48% coefficient of in-breeding in its most intense form. The coefficient of most breeds as bred by regular dog breeders is less than 5%.

"Judging from the usual pedigree, breeders think that they are line-breeding when the same name appears more than once in a four-generation pedigree, even if the repetition appears in the third and fourth generation. The results of our analysis of the Frankie Strain show what most geneticists would predict, namely, that one is not getting any appreciable in-breeding effect when the common contributor comes through an ancestor representing two of sixteen in his generation (one duplication of names in the fourth generation) or two out of eight if the contributor appears twice in the great-grandfather generation. If one had a valuable stud available he would certainly use him as a sire. In line-breeding an even closer relationship is sought. A lesser one will not result in desired inherited effects."

If a foundation sire has the desirable characteristics which the breeder wishes to retain, the breeder must in some way keep the relationship of this desirable individual to the offspring at a more than one-half value. This can be done by bringing together a full line of the breeding stock which has a high representation of the genes of the dog from which the breeder is getting the character traits and the physical traits which he wishes to hold.

By using five hundred and three descendants of Frank of Ledge Acres for analysis of the fetch test scores, Dr. Ginsburg found that the more Frankie genes inherited by the offspring the higher scores they made. By studying the table below we find the results are fantastic. Not only do the puppies improve, but 52% are nearly perfect when Frankie is more closely related to them than if he were their sire. Only 25% qualified for this high score when Frankie was their sire or equivalent.

"Line-breeding to Frankie produced results that are significant by statistical tests," is the scientific way Dr. Ginsburg expresses it.

The following statistical table is Dr. Ginsburg's:

Relationship to Frankie	FETCH SCORES			
	Low 0–1	Medium 2–3	High 4–5	No. of Dogs
Less than sire......	31%	47%	22%	134
Sire or equivalent...	23%	52%	25%	298
More than sire.....	11%	37%	52%	71

Dr. Ginsburg lumped 0–1 (failure and borderline); 2–3 (passed), and 4–5 (near perfect and perfect) to correct the margin of error shown in an analysis of the graders' scores.

Dr. Ginsburg found that the correlation between the scores of parents and their offspring in the fetch test was greatest when parents were less related. Within the line-bred strain the trait comes through even if one of the parents does not show it to a high degree.

"In the sample taken, Fetch Score is significantly related to success in passing the Guide Dog Training. It is also good enough to use as a strong guide in selecting breeding stock at twelve weeks of age. A study of the complete tests is underway both in an effort to determine an even better means of selecting breeding stock and for use in scientific papers to be published later," Dr. Ginsburg reported.

"How is the Fetch Trait inherited? By a complex combination of genes which produce the maximum results through line-breeding."

There are two reasons why the progeny produced by the accumulation of the good genes of one ancestor, selected for his or her excellence, will become uniformly suitable for the purpose for which they are bred: 1) the breeder naturally selects the best specimens from successive litters for continued breeding. These are the individuals that show and transmit the desired traits; 2) the breeder, by eliminating from the breeding program the individuals that show or transmit undesirable traits, screens these traits out of his strain permanently.

The end result is that all dogs in the line possess an inherited predominance of the desired physical and character traits, and can be relied upon to mature into the kind of dog that they were bred to be, and, if bred together, to reproduce dogs with the desirable traits which they themselves possess.

"Proper socialization, handling and training are necessary to realize the potential that exists in even the best strains. On the other hand, superior socialization, handling and training will not make a good Guide Dog out of inferior genetic stock. The successfully trained Guide Dog results oftener and truer from the line-bred individuals of carefully selected stock than from outcrosses of even excellent individuals. One importance of line-breeding is to achieve uniform results," concludes Dr. Ginsburg.

B. K. Miller photo

This litter of 12 closely linebred Frankie strain puppies shows that deleterious effects need not be feared when intelligence is used in selection of breeding stock.

159

Mr. Alvin Kinser, Tallant, Oregon, says, "I trust Timmy, my Labrador retriever Guide Dog to take me over my newspaper route daily. It is he who knows the route. When there are obstructions in our path he takes the responsibility of taking me through, around or even over some new detour. He can even reverse the route and never miss a delivery. On collection days he takes me only to the homes of the monthly subscribers, bypassing the annual subscribers. We deliver 160 newspapers daily and he has never failed me."

CHAPTER XII

Who Will Take Responsibility?

A black Labrador retriever Guide Dog named Timmy helps his blind master carry a 160-paper route.

When James Alvin Kinser, 304 East Main St., Tallant, Oregon, took over a newspaper delivery route in the nearby town of Ashland, the boy who had been carrying the route took him over it for ten days just as he would have taken a sighted person. What was different was that Timmy, Mr. Kinser's Guide Dog, was leading him on the route and learning it for him. After ten trips Mr. Kinser and Timmy took the route on their own and missed only two stops. So the previous carrier returned and took them over it for two more days, showing Timmy where he had missed, and since then the two, man and dog, work the route without a miss. If there are obstructions such as cars parked in their path, roller skates left on the sidewalk, car jacks left in the entrances of commercial garages, or barricades where the sidewalk has been torn up, Timmy and Mr. Kinser deliver their papers and Timmy has to figure out how to get to each delivery place.

How thoroughly Timmy takes the responsibility of making the decisions can be illustrated by the two apartment buildings which stand adjacent and are under the same management. Timmy was taught to climb one flight of stairs, deliver the papers in that apartment and then to go down to the ground floor, cross over to the adjacent building and climb another flight to make deliveries in the second building. There was, however, a catwalk across on the top floor used by personnel. Timmy decided that this could save an extra climb and so crossed over, leading Mr. Kinser safely, and never missed a delivery in the next building, even though he had to reverse the order.

"Whatever Timmy does I accept as the right thing to do," Mr. Kinser says. "That is why I have him, to lead me. Sometimes I get a little bothered when situations become strange, but when I inquire of someone about what has happened, I always find out that there has been a good reason for Timmy making a change."

Timmy takes responsibility. This is one of the most important things in leading the blind. A dog who will not take responsibility is a menace and can easily endanger the life of his master, even leading him into the path of death. For that reason no dog who refuses to take responsibility can be assigned to lead the blind. Often a dog will not show this weakness until it has completed its training. At that time it must lead its trainer under blindfold through all the traffic hazards that the blind master will encounter.

Many dogs who trained well up to this point (even better than most of their classmates) used to become confused when required to lead a blindfolded trainer. The strain of having to exercise independent judgment when they were confronted with unusual experiences in unusual situations was more than they could take.

I have used the words, "used to become confused," deliberately. This was the situation in 1953 when I took all our training and testing records since 1947 with me to Roscoe B. Jackson Memorial Laboratory at Bar Harbor, Maine, to analyze them under the sponsorship of Dr. J. Paul Scott. I had been granted a Guggenheim Fellowship and had been invited to Bar Harbor as a summer investigator to find out what could be done about this situation.

It was one of the toughest problems we have faced in our puppy research, but today we have it almost entirely eliminated.

The problem was especially difficult because the dog who refused to take responsibility was often a dog who scored very high in his training and had shown a high test score. The correlation between his training and test score was almost always excellent. He should have been a top dog both by his training score and his test score. He was also an expensive dog to reject. A trainer had put in the full three-month training period. To all intents and purposes the dog was ready to lead the blind, until under the blindfold test he failed in his last week of training.

An analysis of the data showed that an accidental environmental variable had been introduced and that it was producing important effects on the results in training. This variable was the length of time which the puppy remained in the kennel at San Rafael after the conclusion of the tests and before being delivered to its new home. Of one hundred and twenty-four puppies who had passed the tests, forty were placed in the homes within one week, and twenty-two more within two weeks after they finished their tests. None of the forty failed in training because of refusal to take responsibility; only three of the twenty-two failed. This ties in directly with the Hamilton Station experiments in the effect of early socialization and, probably, with the discovery of the critical periods and their importance to the time when adjustments can best be made.

A population of two hundred and forty-nine puppies was analyzed; all of them had been tested. There were one hundred and eighty-five who passed the tests and sixty-four who failed. Only one hundred and twenty-four of the one hundred and eighty-five were trained. The sixty-one not trained were divided almost equally as follows: 1) best-scored puppies kept for breeding; 2) too small or too large for Guide Dogs at maturity; 3) died before old enough to train. Of the sixty-four who failed the tests, thirty were kept and trained as controls. Identical home care and training were given the controls as were given the puppies who had passed their tests. No one but myself knew which were which, and I had nothing to do with the placing, which was done at random when homes were available. This resulted in a difference in percentage of passed puppies and failed puppies having been placed in the various weeks.

Since the importance of when a puppy should go to a foster home was not known by us at the time, no special effort had been made to have homes available at the right time. Instead, the Farm advisors were advised when puppies were ready, and they found as many 4-H Club member homes as they could as soon as they could. If there were not enough 4-H homes, notices were released to the newspapers that puppy homes were needed and the puppies were thus placed in other homes at various ages. The puppies who remained in the kennel after the completion of the tests received good care but little socialization.

There is naturally some variability in the home rearing. Instructions are given and followed, but since homes and families vary, so the environment varies.

Homes were selected which it was believed would provide the desired environmental conditions. The purpose of the home environment, aside from the fact that social adjustment at an early age was known to be desirable, was to bring the puppy into close association with one child, who gave it some basic training, but principally love and attention, and to have the dog grow up accustomed to traveling in cars and living in a home as it would have to do when it became a Guide Dog.

At about fifty-two weeks of age the dogs are returned to San Rafael for training by staff trainers. Dogs receive three months' training. During this time any dog which shows it will not make a Guide Dog is dropped.

The dogs which would not take responsibility rarely showed that they would not until all training had been completed and they were tested under blindfold.

When the number of weeks which the puppies were left in the kennel awaiting homes, after the conclusion of the tests, was taken into consideration, it was found that of those puppies who had passed their tests and been placed in a home the first week after conclusion of the tests, ninety per cent became Guide Dogs; those who were in the kennel more than a week and less than two weeks fared almost, but not quite, as well; those left in the kennel more than two weeks but less than three showed only about fifty-seven per cent Guide Dogs; of those who were in the kennel more than three weeks after the tests, only thirty per cent became Guide Dogs.

This became increasingly important in our research as we

came to realize that nearly all the dogs that failed to take responsibility were from this group which had been left in the kennel for a considerable length of time after the tests were concluded. The break in socialization seemed to be the cause. It appears that there is a frustration set up by neglecting the puppy at this age which may rob it of the self-reliance needed for it to take responsibility when it matures.

As is considered necessary at Hamilton Station, the data was analyzed for reliability. A comparison of the puppies left in the kennel for more than two weeks after the conclusion of the tests with those placed in puppy homes sooner, using the "chi square" test, gives the probability of obtaining the results we had gotten in training through an accident of random sampling to be less than one in one thousand times. This is such positive proof of the reliability of the data that it may be safely assumed that to leave a puppy in a kennel for a period of more than two weeks without socialization, or, as in this case, to break off socialization which had been conducted for a period of five Thursdays, will have a detrimental effect upon the trainability of this puppy when it becomes an adult dog.

During the last four years the puppies at Guide Dogs for the Blind, who have had to be held over for more than one week after the conclusion of their tests, due to illness or for any reason, have been continued in some of their testing program by the same person who had tested them. The result has further substantiated the conclusions drawn from the above analysis, since these puppies who have been kept socialized during their enforced retention at the kennel have trained almost as well as those who were placed in homes within a week after the tests ended. There have been hardly any of the emotional breakdowns among these puppies which we had been experiencing with the puppies retained without continued socialization—and this though they received socialization but once a week.

Thus, what had seemed to be an unsolvable problem up until 1953 has been solved in two ways: 1) within one week after the puppies have finished their tests, Mrs. Pfaffenberger and I load them into a station wagon and take them directly to the 4-H puppy raisers' homes, where they start getting daily training lessons of fifteen minutes and home care. Many of them attend class under a 4-H leader who is also an obedience dog trainer, and who gives the children and their puppies an hour a week puppy training lessons. Almost none of these puppies fails to make a Guide Dog. 2) We make sure that any puppy who cannot be placed in his puppy home at the conclusion of the tests, or within one week thereafter, is kept socialized. This is done by the puppy testers putting the puppies through some tests and playing with them once a week.

As I have said, the purpose of the study in animal behavior at Bar Harbor is to find out why we behave the way we do. Naturally, a phenomenon such as this break in socialization, with its disastrous effects, is of interest in such a study. There may be implications in what causes the parallel behavior in people. The possibilities have been explored in an article written by Dr. J. Paul Scott and the author, which appeared in the *Journal of Genetic Psychology* in 1959.

By the same token, the many dog folks who have received these articles so enthusiastically may be interested in a new book by Dr. Scott just published by the University of Chicago Press, entitled, *Animal Behavior*. It is written in language which all of us can understand, and covers a very wide field: protozoa to chimpanzees and dogs. It explains many things we have all long wanted to know.

In analyzing the reasons which cause the emotional blocks in adult dog behavior, two hypotheses are suggested: 1) a break in the development of the social relationship causes a consequent emotional disturbance; 2) there is a critical period for learning social behavior and for adjustment from a poor social environment to a rich one.

Dr. Scott also thinks that our form of puppy testing—having so many persons test the puppies and then transferring the puppies to 4-H homes at twelve weeks—may be a sort of conditioning which is good for a dog which will at one year have to adjust to being transferred from his 4-H home to a kennel, and training under a new master, the Guide Dog trainer, and, three months later, being transferred to the blind master.

The following table is a study of the forty-five puppies who

166

passed their puppy tests but failed in training. The table shows the number of weeks they were retained in the kennels after the tests, and the reasons the trainers could not train them to be satisfactory Guide Dogs.

	Number of weeks retained in Kennel after conclusion of tests	
Reason for failure	Less than two	More than two
Refused to take responsibility.............	3	16
Will not train..........................	–	3
Frightened by people, awnings, obstacles....	2	11
Flighty, unstable......................	1	1
Sharp, bites...........................	1	1
Car sick, (cannot overcome it)...........	–	1
Nervous, wetting and defecating..........	–	3
Total................................	7	38

It is also interesting to see how the 25 who failed both the tests and training fared in the same sort of comparison.

Refused to take responsibility.............	–	2
Will not train..........................	4	7
Frightened by people, awnings, obstacles....	3	7
Car sick...............................	–	1
Too soft (over-reacts to corrections)........	–	1
Total................................	7	18

To get as definite a picture as possible of just what happened to all the puppies who were trained, as separated by the tests into the two original groups of passed and failed, we next will study a table first of one hundred and twenty-four puppies who passed the tests according to the number of weeks they were detained in the kennels after the tests, and the passed or failed results when trained for Guide Dogs. Then we will see a table with the same data as it applies to the thirty controls from the group of sixty-four who failed the tests but had identical home care and training.

Placed in Homes after Tests	Became Guides	Failed in Training
(124 puppies who passed test.)		
40 within 1 week...................	36=90%	4=10%
22 within 2 weeks.................	19=86+%	3=13+%
19 within 3 weeks.................	11= 57+%	8=42+%
43 placed after 3 weeks.............	13=30%	30=70%
Total Number....................	79=63+%	45=36+%
(30 puppies selected as controls from 64 who failed tests.)		
6 within 1 week....................	1=16 2/3%	5=83 1/3%
2 within 2 weeks..................	0= 0%	2=100%
9 within 3 weeks..................	4=44 4/9%	5=55 5/9%
13 placed after 3 weeks.............	0= 0%	13=100%
Total Number....................	5=16 2/3%	25=83 1/3%

It is only fair to the testers to explain that they had three puppies whose tests were scored failures, but whose failures they felt were due to illness (the puppies ran a temperature all during the tests) rather than inherited character traits. Because it would upset all calculations if you were to start making exceptions for any reason in such a study, the puppies were recorded "failed" with a notation on the records that the testers did not believe the tests were a true indication of the puppies' abilities. In a final check, after all records were completed and analysis made, these three puppies were found to be among the five from the control goup of thirty "failed puppies" who became Guide Dogs.

Either way you look at the results, the table shows that puppies who failed the tests were likely to fail in training no matter when they were placed in homes, while those who passed the tests suffered a much greater failed percentage if they were kept in the kennel without socialization. The longer they were kept the greater the loss.

CHAPTER XIII

4-H Club's Contribution in Environment, Training and Research

At the outset, we pointed out that the research in animal behavior at Hamilton Station is being carried on to understand why we human beings behave the way we do. They are making a searching investigation into behavior with the hope that we can discover how we can raise our children, or at least our grandchildren, so that they will not suffer from the maladjustments and mental ills so prevalent today.

It seems fitting, then, that a large group of young people, ten to twenty-one years of age, in the 4-H Clubs of California, Oregon, Washington, Nevada, and Utah have contributed very materially to this research: first, by providing a uniform environment for puppies to grow up in, so that a valid study could be made of the puppy tests; second, to make it possible, through this uniform environment, to discover why dogs refuse to take responsibility; third, by proving that they are good enough trainers to be trusted with the early obedience instructions of future Guide Dogs; fourth, by participating in research that is providing data which, when accumulated, may extend our knowledge of dogs (and possibly of people), beyond generally accepted ideas concerning the influence of heredity and environment. It occurs to me that very few of these 4-H youngsters who are aiding in this program will ever have any personal problems with mental health or maladjustment.

Paul C. Barker, 4-H specialist, has kindly assembled a brief historical summary of how this wonderful group of young people happened to become a part of the program. It will be noted that they were a part of the puppy-raising program even before puppy testing started. They have been a very important part of it ever since it began. Mr. Barker has neglected to mention that he was a member of the California 4-H staff that met with Mrs. Walter S. Heller, and at first felt some misgiving about 4-H members raising Guide Dog puppies. Here is how it all came about, as Mr. Barker remembers it.

"On September 17, 1945 the director of the University of California Agriculture Extension Service, in charge of 4-H Club work in California, received a most unusual letter. It came from Mrs. Heller, vice-president of Guide Dogs for the Blind, Inc. In her letter, Mrs. Heller outlined the purpose of her organization and asked the help of California 4-H Club members to provide personal attention and homes at member expense for three-month-old puppies, returning them to Guide Dogs for the Blind, Inc., after nine months for the actual Guide Dog training.

"At first the staff felt some misgiving about this project. We all know it doesn't take long to become attached to a puppy, and it was feared that the sad experience of surrendering a puppy would limit the interest of 4-H members. It was felt, however, if special emphasis were placed upon the importance of the puppy's ultimate purpose in life—service to humanity—there would be ready acceptance. On that basis then, in October 1945, the Guide Dog project was made available to California 4-H Club members living on farms.

"While most 4-H projects bring some economic returns, the Guide Dog project represents a contribution of $80—$100 by each puppy raiser to this philanthropic work. Despite these costs for food and housing, the Guide Dog puppy raising project has grown in popularity until now we have more applications than puppies, even though in one year, August 1, 1957 to August 1, 1958, 4-H Club members in 34 counties of California accepted 153 puppies to raise and 14 club members continued to keep and train and properly care for one brood bitch or stud each, which they had raised for Guide Dogs for the Blind, Inc., for this purpose. Many club members have raised more than one puppy, several as many as six and seven.

"While in the 4-H home, the pup is really a member of the family. He sees strange machines, hears new noises, and meets new people and animals. He goes to 4-H Club meetings and, in many counties, attends classes once a week conducted in each case by a 4-H leader who is also a recognized amateur or professional obedience trainer. The child is provided with a manual in care and training of a Guide Dog puppy and devotes 15 minutes a day at home to obedience training. In August each year the puppy raisers attend a 4-H Guide Dogs Field Day at San Rafael and compete in age classes 3–6 months, 6–9 months, 9–12 months and over 12 months in both obedience and condition-and-showmanship.

"Showing dogs at Field Day follows 4-H Club practice in judging: 1) Every child competes in both classes. 2) Blue ribbons are awarded to the top 30%, red to the next 40%, and green to the bottom 30%. Each dog is individually scored and ribbons are awarded on the basis of the score. 3) An engraved trophy is awarded in obedience and showmanship to the highest scoring dog and handler. 4) Such special work as is being done in research projects such as training for hunting is demonstrated by these Club members and a suitable gift such as a field trial whistle is given each contestant. Guide Dogs' training staff judge the puppies.

"When the puppy is returned to Guide Dogs for the Blind, Inc., for training, his 4-H family waits anxiously for an announcement of his graduation. When possible, they attend the graduation exercises, meet the new master and the puppy raiser presents the puppy officially. Many of the families travel several hundred miles to be present when the dog they have raised graduates. The brief reunion between the puppy raisers and the Guide Dog is always a touching and inspiring event. When the uniformed 4-H member proudly leads his or her dog onto the rostrum for the presentation the applause from the audience shows how sincerely the work done by these youngsters is appreciated.

" 'Of the many projects available to the 4-H Club member, the Guide Dog project is the richest in terms of value in the youngster's development,' according to R. O. Monosmith, State 4-H Club Leader."

As this program advanced it became obvious that the 4-H puppy raiser could, if given a little help, start the puppies in obedience training at thirteen weeks of age and, over a period of nine months, during which they would have the puppies in their homes, so accustom them to such commands as come, sit, stay, fetch, down, down-stay and heel that it would not be necessary for the training staff to spend so much time on obedience training as they had in the past. This would free the trainers' time for more Guide Dog work. Obedience instructions to fit the Guide Dog training were written into a manual: 1) A Guide Dog must lead out so as to pull on the harness. Even on the leash he walks further ahead than is allowed in regular obedience. 2) A Guide Dog never sits in front of his master, but always, on both come and fetch, goes to the right and around behind, then sits at his master's left knee. 3) Guide Dogs fetch on leash.

The puppies are now trained in this manner and the results have been most gratifying. Special Guide Dog 4-H puppy raisers' classes are now being conducted for members of twenty California counties, four Oregon counties, one Nevada, one Washington and one Utah county.

The uniformity of puppy raising and training makes the research studies more reliable than they could be under any other system available to us. Thus, data which made possible the discovery of why a dog fails in taking responsibility, and that line-bred dogs are dependable Guide Dog producers, have been found to be reliable because the 4-H Club members have conscientiously applied the best principles of animal husbandry with exceptionally fine dog training. They also provided a uniform enough environment to make the studies possible.

In his recent book, *Animal Behavior*, Dr. Scott points out: "The study of the socialization process in the dog is complicated by two factors: extreme genetic variability and the fact that socialization takes place readily with either dogs or human beings."

As we have shown in an earlier chapter, it is important that a dog receive the proper amount and kind of socialization with both man and other dogs if he is to be useful. Up to seven weeks of age, a puppy needs canine socialization. At five or six weeks of age he can start his human socialization. When the break comes at weaning, human socialization should be increased, but some canine socialization should continue to make him a well-rounded individual.

Two groups of 4-H puppy raisers are now conducting an experiment for us. One has a litter of five Labradors and the other a litter of six German shepherds. Puppies from identical breedings turned out exceptionally well last year. They are from line-bred strains. These puppies were socialized in our kennels at five and six weeks of age. Without puppy tests, basing their likely potentials on line-breeding and the quality of last year's litters, these puppies were taken into the home at seven weeks of age. They have been started in training at once. The answers we are looking for are: 1) Can our line-bred strains be trusted to produce ninety per cent Guide Dogs without the puppy tests? 2) Will starting puppies in class training at seven weeks of age produce less good, equally good, or better puppies than starting them in class at thirteen weeks of age?

One of our greatest experiments with the aid of 4-H puppy raisers has been with our retrievers. An eighth-grade puppy raiser produced results which got us started on this.

It had always been assumed by our trainers that a sporting dog had so much urge to hunt that, if he were allowed to hunt while a puppy, he would always be a nuisance if trained for other work because he would be so interested in game that even pigeons on the street would cause him to forget the work for which he had been trained. For this reason, for years all puppy raisers who received retrievers were asked not to allow the puppy to hunt under any condition.

Retriever failures ran pretty high and trainers often suspected that the pups had been hunted anyway. Then I met Bev Fletcher and saw what he had done with Lanny, "the old flunker," as he called him.

Lanny is a black Labrador retriever. His tests had been high, but he had not only failed as a Guide Dog, but was so cross with

Bev's friends that he had to be kept tied when they came to visit. The Fletchers live at Janesville, California, where there are plenty of deer (legal to hunt with dogs) on a waterfowl flyway, and where two kinds of quail and pheasants are plentiful. Yet so seriously had Bev and his father taken our request not to allow Lanny to hunt that the dog had never had his nose on any game.

When he failed in his Guide Dog training the Fletchers were asked, as is our custom, if they would like to have Lanny as their own. They wrote, "Bev would like Lanny back and is enclosing an application for another puppy to raise for you." Still convinced that failure in retrievers was traceable to the raisers' having allowed them to hunt, a German shepherd pup, Marco, was sent to Bev this time.

In the summer of 1955, Mrs. Pfaffenberger and I drove to Janesville to bring in Marco, now twelve months of age, and to take the third puppy, Dusty, a Weimaraner, for Bev to raise.

I was impressed with the German shepherd, but I could not get my eyes off Lanny. He was friendly and even looked different. He was very obedient, completely reformed.

This is what had happened. As soon as Lanny came home he was given some training for hunting for the first time in his life, and subsequently had had a full season of hunting all kinds of game. As soon as he was allowed to use his natural urge he changed completely. He now was friendly with those who had not dared go near him before. He showed every sign of wishing to please, a complete contrast to his previous behavior.

In my mind an old belief began to fade. I asked permission to take Lanny back for retraining. I gave Bev permission to hunt Dusty, the Weimaraner pup. (He developed into an excellent hunter, and later into just as fine a Guide Dog.) Because they realized how important such a test might be to Guide Dogs, the Fletchers agreed to let Lanny return for retraining.

Lanny's scores on his retraining were so significant that our policy concerning the proper way to raise a sporting dog puppy to be a Guide Dog has been exactly reversed.

Here is how Lanny scored on (1) Puppy Tests; (2) Before being hunted; (3) After a season of hunting:

174

	Puppy Tests (1)	Trainers' Scores (2)	Trainers' Scores (3)
Come	4	2	3
Sit	5	2	4
Fetch	4	1	4
Eye Test	3	1	2
Intelligence	4	0	2
Willingness	4	0	4

Lanny failed the second time, but not because of his grades. He was one of those unfortunate puppies who were kept in the kennel too long after the tests (for eight weeks). He failed because he could not take responsibility. He did not become a Guide Dog, but today we ask sporting breed raisers not to do only one thing, namely, not to train on pigeons.

For the first three years our class for hunting breeds, which teaches the puppies to hunt under the expert tutelage of field-trialer Val Dervin of Stockton, has produced but one failure in Guide Dog training. Many of the dogs from this class get in a full season on game. None that has been hunted has failed in Guide Dog training.

Naturally we are running control groups, and we hope soon to have enough data to publish significant results. It is my personal opinion that a dog, like a human, can have urges so great that to be denied the right to exercise them may cause such frustrations that he cannot do any work well. This can be much more true with dogs that have been bred for many generations from ancestors with character traits which have been emphasized through gene selection to a point where their characteristic breed activities are practically, if not exactly, purely instinctive.

Dr. Scott has watched the development of the parallel studies at Roscoe B. Jackson Memorial Laboratory and Guide Dogs for the Blind, and he read and approved each of these chapters before it was published. He has authorized us to quote his evaluation of the 4-H Guide Dogs puppy raising program as follows:

"One of the biggest problems in the training of dogs is that they have to receive their final education as adults, but as we

175

have shown with our experiments, the puppy actually begins to learn at approximately three weeks of age. Anything he learns from this time on is likely to affect his performance as an adult. Your aim should be to give the puppy the kind of experience which will make him a good learner in the future and to avoid the kind of experience which will interfere with learning. The chief function of the 4-H program is to provide the dog with a rich and stimulating atmosphere in which he is constantly learning new things. Thus, when he comes back to be trained he will be ready to keep on learning the things required of a Guide Dog.

"Our studies and those made at Guide Dogs for the Blind, Inc., have also shown that keeping a dog in a barren kennel environment teaches him a habit of not learning, and anything like this should be avoided in the 4-H home. The puppy raiser should particularly avoid keeping the dog closely confined, or subject to a narrow routine of existence. Anything that the puppy can learn while in his 4-H home should be good unless it would directly interfere with Guide Dog performance (as, for example, the pursuit of pigeons).

"One thing we would like to know more about is the best way to transfer a dog from the kennel to his home environment. This is emotionally upsetting to the puppies, but you want them to be able to do this so that they will be able to stand it again when they are taken from the 4-H home to be trained for Guide Dogs. We believe that there is probably an ideal time around the twelfth week of age. Doing it sooner may be so upsetting that the puppy becomes more dependent on the puppy raiser and less able to leave him afterward. Taking him from his litter mates earlier, around seven weeks, is ideal for many dog owners but not for a dog that must be able to make several changes from one master to another. We also believe that the way in which the transfer is done is important, and that one of the things the puppy testing program does is to give the puppy practice in moving out of the kennel.

"Finally, we cannot emphasize too much the importance of good genetic stock. We have shown that there are big differences between dogs in the tendency to develop inhibitions, or to learn not to learn. The ideal Guide Dog has to be a quick and ready learner, both positively and negatively, and it looks as if progress is being made in selecting these dogs."

Mrs. Nathan (Virginia) Beauchamp, who is one of the outstanding Amateur Obedience Trainers who donates her time and her whole heart to conducting one of the 4-H puppy training classes for Guide Dog puppy raisers, has kindly consented to let us include the following tribute written by her about one of her 4-H class members at the time of the child's tragic death.

THE THIRD PUPPY

"Do you ever get a peculiar hunch about a certain pup? Does he have a wee bit of extra tilt to his head when spoken to, or does he handle himself in a specially fine way as he plays, or perhaps there's something about him you'd rather not even try to explain? Of course you do.

"And this is doubly true in the guide dog puppy obedience classes, where the 4-H youngsters, whose project is raising a puppy for Guide Dogs, train their charges in simple obedience and the ways of life. Given an extra special set of hand-picked pups matched with an extra special set of 4-H kids—and those spine-tingling hunches really vibrate. These pups plus these boys and girls add up to good!

"Clarence J. Pfaffenberger, vice-president of Guide Dogs for the Blind, Inc., in San Rafael, California, and man in charge of the school's puppy testing and placement program, has said, 'It is a fact that in 1957 94% of the puppies from our selected breeding stock (selected from breeding by our puppy tests) and raised by 4-H members became Guide Dogs. When we started the program of testing and placing in 4-H homes, we trained 109 dogs one year to get 9 Guide Dogs. Of course, 4-H has not made the entire difference, testing has not made the entire difference, but between the two a lot has been done. Research has proved that a puppy needs a child just in the same way a child needs a puppy. Dogs raised in a kennel without the feeling of being needed and appreciated grow up to be worthless, especially for Guide Dogs. The important thing is that puppies properly raised in the homes are so far superior to anything that

177

could be produced under kennel conditions that the blind students receive dogs socially adjusted to be dependable eyes for them, dogs who delight in serving.'

"So it was really a thrill for us as 4-H leaders and dog fanciers to have one of our 4-H youngsters, 13 year old Susan Nicholson of St. Helena, California, apply for her third puppy to raise. Susan's first puppy project had been black Labrador, Winnie. No one could ever forget Winnie, and even now that she is a well-behaved, much admired, full-fledged Guide, visions keep returning of the energetic, irresponsible, fun-loving pup she once was. Though Winnie's mind worked like lightning, Susan and she were well matched. Perhaps they both sharpened their wits together as they both learned so fast. After Winnie was returned to the School for serious adult Guide training, Babs, a woolly Golden Retriever, came home to live with Susan. Babs attended weekly obedience class just as had Winnie, and in no time at all, it seemed, tearful goodbyes were said to her as she, too, returned to School where she is now in training. But Susan's application was already in the Guide Dog file for another pup, the third one.

"When she met her newest charge, Susan's grin had been a mile wide, while three months old Golden Retriever, Andy, wriggled himself into position for a joyous poke at Susan's cheek with his wet, black nose. And then, even as the stage was set for a happy reenactment of past puppy projects, tragedy stalked the wings, dropping the curtain, suddenly and violently.

"A few days later Susan was gone—she and her father killed in a grinding highway crash the day after Christmas.

"Shocked and stunned, the little community of St. Helena recovered, and poured out its sympathy in word and deed to the remaining family—mother and four children. And as Susan had been a shining example of leadership and progress in her school and club work, so had her father been in community life. They were both admired, loved and respected. Wishing her love for Guide Dog puppies not to be ended, only well begun, Susan's friends proposed a memorial be established in her memory. They appealed to Mr. Pfaffenberger for help in phrasing this memorial, in view of her interest in the puppy testing and training program. This is the Memorial which will be represented by a plaque on the grounds of the Guide Dogs for the Blind School:

SUSAN HALE NICHOLSON MEMORIAL

Established by Her Napa
County Friends

The purpose of this memorial is to inaugurate a Research Endowment Fund to carry on and expand the puppy research and puppy raising program, to the improvement of which Susan Hale Nicholson and her fellow 4-H Club members have generously contributed their time, their skill, their money and their love.

"This is the first time research for Guide Dogs has been sponsored, except for the Fellowship given Mr. Pfaffenberger by the Guggenheim Foundation several years ago. . . . And through the combined efforts of Guide Dogs for the Blind, in its research work, and the Roscoe B. Jackson Memorial Laboratory, Bar Harbor, Maine, further progress in pure scientific research in dogs is promised. When it is properly evaluated, the valuable, accumulated data will be made available to the dog fanciers through publications, as it was in 1958 in a series of ten articles in *Pure Bred Dogs*, entitled 'Science Has a New Look at Behavior.'

"So, as her 4-H companions continue with their projects of puppy raising, Susan will keep pace through the Memorial Research Fund, enabling not only more and better puppies for Guide Dogs, but more and better knowledge for dog breeders and mankind everywhere.

"Yes, Susan would very much approve."

In closing, I should like to remind all that every summer about thirty high school and thirty college students who are talented in the fields of science are selected from throughout the United States to live and work with the savants from many parts of the world who gather at Jackson Laboratory to search for scientific truths. How fitting it would be if one or more of the sterling 4-H puppy raisers were chosen to spend three months in this stimulating climate of ideas. I sincerely hope that one or more of them may be fortunate enough to travel down the winding Eden road to the gap in the forest which reveals the unbelievable blue of Frenchman's Bay, and then turn in through the stone gate to Hamilton Station for an inspiring summer.

CHAPTER XIV

How to Raise Your Guide Dog Puppy

The following is the manual the 4-H Guide Dog puppy raisers use to raise the most perfect Guide Dogs we have ever had:

Good health and normal growth are as important in the proper development of a good dog as they are in that of any animal. If you carefully follow these instructions, your puppy should keep well and strong and grow up to be a blue ribbon Guide Dog prospect.

You have been entrusted with a purebred puppy from highly selected breeding stock of a strain developed especially by Guide Dogs for the Blind, Inc., to lead sightless people. Guide Dogs for the Blind, Inc., does not hold you or your parents legally liable for your dog, but every dog lost to the program causes a break in the plans to provide as many dogs as possible.

This puppy has been selected by special aptitude tests which show that it is superior in the natural tendencies which every Guide Dog must inherit. Every effort has been made by the Guide Dog School to deliver this puppy to you in fine physical condition, and with its training enough advanced so that with a daily fifteen-minute training period, you will have a well-behaved dog from the start.

Before Your Puppy Comes

1. Build a bed or sleeping box.
2. Get a light chain with at least one swivel in it.
3. Provide a suitable dish for his feed and one for his water.
4. Be sure that your yard fence is dog-tight, or build a run.
5. Provide yourself with a stiff brush and a comb. The kind of brush used for stock and a curry comb are O.K.

After Your Puppy Arrives

1. Let him have time to relieve himself before you take him into the house. Choose the place you want him to go and take him there right away, so he will accept this as his toilet place.
2. Water and feed him and then let him rest.
3. Start training the second day without fail. Teach the four basic exercises from the first: Heel, Sit, Come, Fetch. If there are classes for Guide Dog puppy raisers near your home, you are urged to attend.
4. Use the leash and collar which are provided.

HEALTH, SAFETY AND HAPPINESS

Prevention Shots

Your puppy has had its shots for prevention of distemper and hepatitis, but not rabies. At six months of age, have your veterinarian do this and send the bill to Guide Dogs for the Blind, Inc., San Rafael, California. This does not mean that he cannot take these diseases. He should not be knowingly exposed to any disease.

Your puppy has been wormed, but sometimes dogs get reinfested. Should you suspect worms, follow your veterinarian's advice.

Veterinarian Can Help

If your puppy becomes ill, call your veterinarian and ask his advice. If necessary, take the puppy to his office.

In all cases when it is necessary to consult a veterinarian about the puppy's health, write Mr. William F. Johns, Executive Director, Guide Dogs for the Blind, Inc., San Rafael, California. In emergency, call him at Glenwood 4-5454. If Mr. Johns cannot be reached, or it is some matter you wish to discuss with the author, write to Clarence J. Pfaffenberger, 1446 Fifteenth Avenue, San Francisco 22, California, or telephone Overland 1-4467.

If your puppy is a female, place her in a veterinarian kennel as soon as she comes in season, and leave her for three weeks. DO NOT HAVE HER SPAYED! Guide Dogs will pay the board bill.

A Run for Your Puppy

A fenced yard or run from which the pup cannot escape is essential to his safety. No valuable dog should ever be allowed to run where he is likely to be hit by a car.

Dogs need mental exercise as well as physical exercise. The old idea that a dog should have a quarter section to run on at will has long been abandoned. Today we know that a dog which is given fifteen minutes of brisk training once or twice a day, and a lot of love and understanding, can live the remainder of the day comfortably in his yard and in your house.

When you are in a safe place like the woods or a large field, let your puppy enjoy a good run. Run and romp with him, but do not leave him to his own ideas about what to do and where to go. Never let him chase stock or poultry. A few fine puppies have been shot by neighbors of the puppy raisers because the puppy raisers had neglected to keep their dogs under control, and the neighbors found them chasing stock and poultry. When you are through with play, put the leash on the puppy and lead him home.

If you do not have a fenced yard, then a run should be constructed, at least six or eight feet wide and fifteen to twenty feet long. If you put him in this when you first get him, you will not need anything heavier than turkey wire to keep him in. To let him get big before you build his run will mean that you may have to use heavy wire and a higher fence, and still have trouble keeping him in. So, start right.

Naturally a puppy should not be left out in bad weather. A good shelter should be provided to shade him from hot sun or rain. A bed in a dry, draft-free room should always be used for him at night and on bad days.

Let Him Grow Up With the Family

While your dog is growing up, you should take him in the house, take him in the car to town but on the leash, and let him become accustomed to people and traffic. In the car, he should sit or ride on the floor, never on the seat. Encourage him to be friendly with people and also with other dogs. Your club leader may want you to bring him to 4-H Club meetings. You may be asked to appear at service club meetings with him, and at school exercises. Always keep him on a leash at such affairs and always keep him under your control. Your classmates will want to play with him, but an inexperienced handler might upset the good work it has taken you weeks to accomplish, or let him loose in a dangerous area where he could be injured or killed.

Cleanliness Is Important

Dogs do not need frequent bathing. Their hair needs the natural oil which soap and water removes. Mostly, a dog can be kept very clean by a daily brisk brushing. This is better than washing. If a puppy gets soiled, it is usually on a limited area of his body. This may be cleaned off by the use of a damp cloth. If bathing is necessary, be careful to avoid getting water and soap in the eyes. A little cotton tucked in each ear before washing and removed just as soon as you finish washing will keep the water from running into the ears.

Ears should be kept clean. A damp cloth will be all you need to wash out the puppy's outer ear. This should be done at least once a week. Dirty ears cause many troubles and encourage ear mites. The ears can become so seriously infested that there is no cure and it may be necessary to have a dog destroyed. So, wiping out with a damp cloth each week is very important.

The eyes should be kept clean, also, by wiping with a damp cloth. If they are injured, or show a discharge, a veterinarian should be consulted. Allowing a puppy to ride with his head out of a car window can cause serious eye injury.

Each August, a Guide Dogs for the Blind Field Day is held at San Rafael. The way you have kept your puppy groomed throughout the year, the cleanness of his ears and eyes will help to win a blue ribbon or maybe a trophy, besides benefiting the puppy's health.

SIMPLE OBEDIENCE TRAINING

The Secret of Successful Dog Training

All of the successful dog trainers, amateur or professional, know the secret and use it. If you, too, use it, training your puppy will be easy; it will be fun; and your puppy will learn quickly.

What is this secret? Just two words—"Be Consistent." Always use the same word for the same command. Always require your puppy to do the same thing in the same way.

This secret of consistency applies to all the training you will do with your puppy. In feeding, select convenient morning and evening hours—let's say 7:00 a.m. and 5:00 p.m. Stick to these hours. Abrupt changes will confuse your puppy, affect his regular habits of elimination, and may make him sick. Be consistent.

In training your puppy to heel, sit, come and fetch, always use the same commands, insist on proper obedience, correct him until he performs correctly, and praise him when he obeys. In this way you are being consistent.

If you take your puppy into the house after playing with him outdoors, and he still wants to play, insist on good house behavior. Attach the leash, and make him heel, sit and stay. In this way he learns correct manners, and will be loved and accepted by your family. This is being consistent.

. A well-mannered Guide Dog reflects your consistent attention to details. You train him to stay off furniture, beds, and automobile seats. He is not fed tidbits from the table. He does not jump on people. He is prevented from fighting. Your early training, followed up by the training he will receive when you return him to the Guide Dogs for the Blind, will help make him into a well-mannered, obedient companion for his sightless master.

Be consistent in your demands, in your correction, and in your praise.

Don't ask your puppy to do anything that it cannot do.

Don't ask your puppy to do anything you cannot make it do.

Praise, the Best Reward

Praise, stroking, and petting are the best rewards you can give a puppy for minding. Never punish a puppy. You can correct him if you are present when he does something wrong. Scolding and preventing him from going ahead with the wrong thing will have the desired effect. If a dog needs punishment, someone is to blame for allowing him to develop a bad habit.

Never Tease a Puppy

It is not necessary to tell a 4-H Club member never to tease a dog. It is possible that someone who does not know this may visit you at some time. If so, be very firm. Impress your visitor that this dog is valuable, that he is becoming a Guide Dog, that teasing makes any dog mean, and that a mean dog can never be trusted with a blind person. Guide Dogs should be friendly with everyone. An overprotective dog is not suitable to be a guide.

This Is How You Housebreak Your Puppy

Guide Dogs have to live in the house with their masters. It is very important that they be housebroken at an early age. Housebreaking a puppy is quite simple, and it is a very fine accomplishment on the part of the puppy raiser.

Here is how you do it. Make a simple bed of plywood or other wood. A wooden box can be made to suit this purpose. Because your pup will grow very fast, it is better to make the bed large enough for him when he is grown. There should be three sides at least ten or twelve inches high to cut out any draft. The fourth side should be open. The floor of the bed should be smooth so that nothing will injure the dog while he lies on it. A plywood bottom gives just enough to be comfortable for a dog. Legs should hold the bed at least three inches off the floor, allowing for circulation underneath.

By inserting an "eye" screw in the wall behind the bed, the

185

puppy may be secured with a light chain, about one and one-half times as long as your puppy. This allows the puppy to get off the bed, but not very far. It allows him complete freedom while on the bed. The chain should have a least one swivel to avoid fouling. After the puppy has been taken outside at bed-time and allowed to eliminate, place him on the bed, snap the chain into his collar ring, and let him sleep there.

Stay with the puppy when you put him out until he has eliminated. If you let him out alone he is likely to want to come in before he has eliminated, just to be with you. As to leaving him out a couple of hours before bedtime, here again you have no assurance he has eliminated. If you have him inside at least an hour before bedtime and take him out, he is almost sure to eliminate quite quickly. Do not rush him. Most dogs' bowels move at least twice before they have completed elimination.

A dog likes to eliminate in the same area where he has gone before, that is, he chooses a place for his toilet. By taking him directly to this place, you will save much time in elimination. If he has an accident in the house, take a little sand or soil, mix it with the eliminated matter, take this soil where you want the dog to "go" and leave it there. You will have told him this is where you want him to eliminate. Take him back to this place when you want him to "go" and you will soon establish this habit. Be sure to wipe the spot clean with some disinfectant so he will not return to this spot in the house to eliminate.

The bed may be used at any time that you want the puppy in the house but do not want him to wander around. It is also quite simple to teach him the word "bed." Call his name and say, "bed," every time you want him on the bed. If you do this before feeding and then feed him directly in front of the bed, you will speed up the learning process. Do not leave food sitting around. Clean up any that falls on the floor. Leptospirosis, a deadly disease, is almost always found to come from dogs picking up food over which rodents have run and urinated. Naturally, the bed should never be used as punishment, nor should the dog be kept there day and night. Housebreaking may be accomplished just as well on a back porch, a sun room, even a harness room in the barn.

186

Leash Can Mean a Good Time

The puppy is delivered to you with his leash and collar. Leave the collar on him at all times. Let out a hole as he grows. If he outgrows the collar, measure it and send in the measurement to Guide Dogs for the Blind, Inc., San Rafael, California, Attn: Mrs. Elizabeth Bancroft, and ask for a larger collar.

Chain training collars should not be used on puppies under six months of age. If the puppy is properly trained according to this manual, he will be so well educated by the time he is six months of age that a chain training collar will be unnecessary.

By putting the leash on the puppy to take him with you and to bring him home, you teach him to associate the leash with a good time. Talk to him as you walk along, as you would talk with a child. He will not understand all you say, but he will enjoy the attention and eventually will understand many words.

You will use the leash only when you are training the pup, or taking him for a walk or a ride. Do not tie him up with it or let him run dragging it. Leave it on when you take him for a ride in an automobile as a safety measure for his control.

Your leash has a loop in one end and a snap on the other. Snap it on the collar ring and hook the loop over your right thumb, letting the leash fall across the palm of your right hand, and grasp it. Fold any excess length in your hand. Keep it as slack as possible and encourage the puppy to walk with you where you want to go. If he wants to go another way at first, walk his way a little, encourage him, and when he is started, go your own direction and he will follow. Soon you will have the puppy walking with the leash hanging slack and his shoulders about even with or a little ahead of your left knee. This is the way he should heel as a future Guide Dog.

Training Your Puppy to "Heel"

Your puppy has not been taught his name. This you will have the privilege of teaching him. Always address the puppy by his name. For instance, say "Roger," count three under your breath to give him time to respond and give you his attention. Then, give the command such as "Heel," "Sit," or "Come."

187

Before you give your puppy the command "Heel," have him sit at your left side. He must sit close with his head straight to the front. He has had a lesson a week in this for five weeks during his tests and already heels pretty well.

When you are ready to start, get his attention by calling his name. When he looks up at you, command "Heel," and at once step forward at a brisk pace with your left foot, always your left foot first. Walk as fast as you can, keeping your pup close to your side with his shoulders even with your left knee or just a little ahead of it, but not enough ahead to cause him to try to cross over in front of you. Go forward, make right turns, left turns and about turns. While you are teaching him, talk to him and encourage him by telling how well he is doing. If he does wrong, say "No," and show him what you want him to do.

Here are some tips about those turns you are making. Many people make awkward turns and foul their dog up in the leash or cause him to tighten the leash, because they do not give him a chance to come around with them. Try this—when you do a right turn, do it when your left foot is out in front in a normal step and your right foot is still touching the ground. Raise up on both toes and pivot to your right. This will give your pup time to come around and continue with you at a regular pace. When you have made a turn, keep on walking.

To do an about-turn, pivot on your toes "right about face" exactly the same way but turn completely around, so you are facing in the opposite direction.

To do a left turn, you still do it when your left foot is out front, but use your right knee to spin you around as a counterbalance. A little shove with your right foot starts you around; the weight of your right leg held up with knee forward carries you to a left face. The knee also block the progress of your pup so that he has to turn with you.

Practice these turns by yourself in your yard or a large room until you have them down pat. Once you can do them well without your puppy, start using them in heeling your pup. Each time you stop, which should be quite often, call your puppy's name and say firmly "Sit." Make sure that your puppy does sit.

Teaching the "Sit" Command

While being tested, your puppy has also been taught to sit. This is the way he was taught. Put your left hand across your puppy's hips so he can sit on it. Place your right hand on his chest. Now push each hand toward the other and call his name and say, "Sit." It is best to kneel by the puppy with him on your left side. The tester taught your puppy to sit by first removing her right hand from his chest leaving only the left hand on his hips. She held her right hand six or eight inches above his eyes and made a downward motion as she gave the command "Sit." Next, she used only her right hand to signal and removed her left hand from his hips.

You can try holding your right hand over his eyes, palm down, six or eight inches from them, and giving the command. If the puppy does not obey, it is likely because you are strange to him, so return to the same method described above and teach him that he must also mind you. Soon he will learn to sit on either the hand signal or command. Once your puppy is minding your "Sit" command, have him sit every time you start an exercise and every time you stop one, always on your left.

When you have stopped and your puppy is in the sitting position on your left side, give the command, thus, "Roger, Stay." You should always carry your leash in your right hand. This leaves your left hand free to perfect the "Stay" command.

This is how you do it. As you give the command, make the left turn just as when heeling, but on the command "Stay" place your left hand directly in front of the puppy's nose with the palm toward him and hold it there while you pivot with your right knee swinging to block his forward progress, should he try to go ahead. You will stop directly in front of your puppy. Withdraw your left hand gently so as not to cause him to move, stand there a short time, then walk directly to his right side, holding the leash loosely, and stop in the same position from which you started. As soon as you have returned, get down on your knee and praise the puppy with petting and kind words.

After a day or two of this, you can back a step away from your pup, after you have turned to face him. His leash should be held loosely.

189

You should now have him sitting steady while you back away as far as possible, still holding the leash. Stand there a short time. If, after seven or eight days' training, he does not move when you back away two or three steps, you are doing very well. If he does move, bring the leash up sharply under his chin and say, "Stay," and go through it as before. Now, instead of holding the leash, lay it over his back. By the time you have progressed to where you can back ten steps away with your pup steady, he should stay without your turning in front of him. Simply give the command "Stay," and walk straight away from him.

Here is a tip. While teaching heeling, you have always started with your left foot making the first step. He has learned to follow that foot. So now, when you leave him, step off always with your right foot. You can still hold your hand in front of his face when you leave him, but walk straight away ten steps, stop and turn to face him. After a while, time yourself and be sure that he will remain sitting while you are away for at least one full minute. When you return to him, always come directly to his right side, exactly where you left him. Stand there for a little while so he will remain steady, then praise him.

Teaching Him to "Come"

Once you have the "Sit-Stay" training accomplished, you will be ready to practice your "Come" exercise. At first, start just as you did on the "Stay." With leash attached to his collar, "Stay" your puppy and walk to the end of the leash, turn and face him, and, after a short interval, command, "Roger, Come." Make this command a very pleasant, happy one, and if he hesitates, because of his "Stay" training, bring him to you gently with the leash, encouraging him all the time.

As he comes to you, you will have to help him. Pulling gently on the leash, bring him to your right side and turn around with him making a right-about turn. This way you lead him back to your left side. Have him sit there for a little while and then praise him. Three or four lessons a day will be all you should give of this exercise. Continue until he minds all these commands without any help from the leash or from your turning.

Once this is accomplished, you may leave him at "Stay" without any leash on him. First, stop about where you have been stopping, while your leash limited the distance you could go away from him. Day by day, go a step farther until you are a full ten steps from him. If he is not letter-perfect at any time, go back to using the leash and working the shorter distance.

(Note: Many of us in obedience training have our dogs come to heel in a different manner from that described here. The reason we ask you to use this type of "finish" is that a Guide Dog must go from right to left behind the blind person so that it will not trip its master.)

Pet him when he comes. Do not trust him to come if he is in danger. It takes a long while to teach him to come so that he will always obey at once when called. Even you sometimes find other things you want to do before coming when you are called. Allow time for the puppy, but continue until you succeed.

Teach Retrieving from the First Day

We have found it actually easier to train Guide Dogs if puppies are given some experience in the field on natural game. NO PIGEONS SHOULD EVER BE USED IN TRAINING.

Any of the breeds, including the Shepherds, seem to benefit from being taught to retrieve from the water. Swimming is good exercise and a puppy that learns to fetch an object to hand from the water soon brings it more readily to the handler even on land.

A Guide Dog must pick up and bring to his master any object he drops. It is desirable for him to enjoy carrying things in his mouth. Your puppy has been given retrieving lessons, but constant practice is necessary. You should give him daily retrieving lessons from the day you get him. A dog toy or ball in his yard will encourage him to carry. However, do not use this for the retrieving object during his lessons, because it is his toy.

Roll up a discarded felt hat and put some adhesive tape· around it to hold it. It will have your scent. It is light, and easy on his teeth. Get very excited about this "precious thing." First show it to him. Encourage him to try to grab it, then throw it a short distance. If he does not retrieve it at once, run after it

191

yourself and pick it up. He will soon want to beat you to it. It may take several days before he enters in the play. When he does pick it up, call "Roger—Come," and start running away from him. When he follows with the hat, slow down gradually until you are even with each other. While speaking to him softly and praising him, slip one arm around him, place your other hand under his chin, and remove the hat from his mouth gently, saying "Roger—Out." Then praise him profusely. Retrieve once the first day, twice the next and increase gradually up to ten, never more. Make it play.

To polish off the training, teach him to come to you with the old rolled up felt hat, sit as he does in the "Come" exercise, on your left side, and let you take the hat out of his mouth gently, without a struggle. Say "Roger, Out." Then praise your puppy.

In both the "Come" and the "Retrieving" exercises, once Roger has learned to come around to your left side on the command "Heel," do not step forward; stand still and have him "Heel."

Should your puppy not want to fetch the old hat directly to you, have him retrieve it on the leash so that he must come to you. As a Guide Dog he will always retrieve on the leash.

Jumping on People

Dogs should not be allowed to jump on people. The best way to prevent it is to teach the pup the word "No." Whenever the pup jumps on any member of the family, the person being jumped on should take the pup's front paws in his hands and gently step on its hind toes while commanding "No." Do this every time and in a week the habit should be broken so that only the word will be necessary to prevent any future attempts. We teach the blind students to use the word "No" as a corrective word because the words "Stay" and "Down" are used in the obedience exercises and each has its own meaning.

FEEDING INSTRUCTIONS

Feed at Regular Times

Feed your puppy morning and evening. An early evening feeding is advisable so that the puppy will have time to eliminate before bedtime. For the first five days, feed kibble only. Use the food and the feeding instructions which are given you when you get your puppy. After two days, start adding meat or meat trimmings from the table and a teaspoon of bacon drippings if if you have them. We feed a half-pound of ground cooked meat daily, but if more convenient, canned horse meat is satisfactory. To this add a teaspoon of Vionate and a teaspoon of cod liver oil once a day. If the meat is added to the dry kibble and mixed with it before the hot broth or water is poured over it, the food will have a better flavor.

A poached egg twice a week instead of the meat is very satisfactory. Raw eggs are half lost because the dog passes the raw white as waste.

Canned fish may be substituted for meat. Mackerel is very good, but never give the puppy home-cooked or raw fish because of the danger of getting bones in his throat.

The same applies to chop, chicken, and steak bones, which splinter. Cooked large bones are bad because they cause compaction in the intestines. While pups like to chew on large, raw leg bones, they are not necessary to their welfare. If you have a dog of your own besides the puppy, you may start a dog fight by feeding bones.

You can judge the amount of food the puppy should have each feeding by the amount he cleans up in 15 minutes. If he leaves food, cut down the amount. If he cleans it up quickly, add a little until you are feeding all he will eat. He should always have as much as he will eat twice daily until he is twelve months of age. Take his dish away after 15 minutes and wash it. By the age of nine or ten months, if your puppy does not eat readily when given his second meal, this will indicate that one meal a day is sufficient.

Enough clean, cool water must be provided daily so that the puppy can have all he wants at any time.

Your Puppy Likes Clean Dishes, Too

Your puppy's feed dish should be washed and scalded after each meal to prevent algae or fungus poisoning. Scrub and scald the water dish at least once a week.

In Case of Diarrhea

For a mild case of diarrhea, give one tablespoon of Kaopectate four times daily. This can be purchased at any drug store. Withhold meat from the food and give no milk while diarrhea persists. If you do feed milk with the other food, give it after the regular meal and not as a full meal.

Sleep your puppy in a warm dry place free from draft, and feed at regular times.

AFTER YOUR PUPPY LEAVES

At about one year of age the puppy you have raised will go back to Guide Dogs for the Blind, Inc., in San Rafael, California. Here it will be assigned to one of the young men who are professional Guide Dog trainers. All the good you have taught it by following this manual and the instructions of your leader will have a great influence upon the success of the specialized training your puppy will now receive. It will even help the dog to be a better dog than it could have been without your help.

Usually, someone from the school will come for your puppy. It may be the trainer who will train it or Mr. and Mrs. Pfaffenberger. Only where distances are too great, weather is too bad, or when there is only one dog in a community is the dog brought in by common carrier, and then by air, if possible.

As soon as your puppy arrives at the school, he has his own kennel where he is isolated for about two weeks from other dogs by a partition inside and wire outside. This is to protect him from taking any disease which another dog might bring in and to protect the other new dogs from anything he might bring into the kennel. During this time he is placed into training, usually the day after he arrives, and so is not kept in the kennel except at night and when not at work.

The reason we cannot tell you exactly how long it will be from the time your puppy comes back to Guide Dogs until it will graduate is that we never know. So many things can happen. If a dog develops an illness or lameness after he starts training, he may be out of his class long enough to have to wait for the next trainer. Even after he has completed his training, he may not be suited to the personality of any member of the class of blind people who come in for training and so may have to wait over for a later class. Thus, through no fault of his own, a dog may be in training several months before he finds his proper niche. Even after that his blind master may get sick and have to go home without a dog and, thus, the process of placing your puppy starts all over again.

We have so many letters and phone calls asking, "Why did Johnny's dog graduate two months ago and mine hasn't graduated yet? I know my dog was smarter than Johnny's."

For this reason we have thought the above information necessary. Usually your puppy will graduate within five months after it returns to Guide Dogs for the Blind, Inc., but if it takes longer, that fact is not an indication that either you or the puppy have failed.

If a puppy fails in training we notify you at once and ask if you wish to have it returned to you as your own dog.

As soon as we feel sure that your puppy is going to graduate, we invite you to come to present him to his new master at the graduation. We send the invitation at least one week before graduation, or as early as we can be sure.

CHAPTER XV

What Will We Do Next?

We feel fortunate that we do not have to stop here in our research. Although, with the exception of the $4,000 Fellowship granted me in 1954 and 1955 by John Simon Guggenheim Memorial Foundation, no funds have been available for our program, my wonderful group of thirty volunteers and the unselfish, patient help of Drs. Scott, Fuller and Ginsburg have made fifteen years of fruitful research possible. The results are that today we have a tremendous volume of data which needs analysis; much of it already points to lines of study which should prove most worthwhile.

The Susan Hale Nicholson Memorial Fund given us to encourage us to try for greater things gave us something to dream about. Then the Salinas Valley Kennel Club sent us $200 to urge us on. The two funds provided means to explore the possibilities of grants which would make it possible to use the data we had, and to go on to explore new fields.

In September, 1960, we went East and, together with Drs. Scott, Fuller and Ginsburg, planned a course which we hoped would bring the financial aid we needed to establish a full-fledged scientific investigation of the things which were evident, and those which only suggested important values.

Our proposals have resulted in two grants which have enabled us to set up a five-year research program at Guide Dogs for the

Blind, with a full-time scientific associate and the counseling services of Drs. Scott, Fuller and Ginsburg at San Rafael each year. To combine a scientific research program with a practical dog breeding and training program will not be easy, but we believe that it can be done to the benefit of all. The fact that our dogs are bred from generations of dogs with carefully recorded production, test, training and service data means adding a new dimension in canine research.

The five-year program we are starting upon is being financed by two grants, both of which we feel were given because of the merit of the research accomplished and to be attempted, and so we feel highly complimented. We estimated that it would cost us, working at the very minimal outlay, $138,000 to do the five-year study. Guide Dogs for the Blind furnishes the dogs and the office space and equipment, and I continue to donate my time except for a brief period each year when my entire attention will be given to the councils. The James Irvine Foundation, San Francisco, made a grant of $5,000, and the United States Department of Health, Education and Welfare has supplied the remainder.

Like everyone else, we have been subjected to warnings from those who were caught up recently in the hip dysplasia hysteria. Over the more than twenty-five years I have been in dogs seriously there have been many hysterias: undershot jaws, overshot jaws, shyness, cowhocks, and many more. I have learned that any defect in an otherwise valuable animal can be bred out in his or her descendants.

We had spent years producing Guide Dogs who would render the kind of service to our students that was most desirable. We had had practically no trouble with lameness in our trained dogs. Occasionally we had lameness in puppies from five to seven months of age. We decided that we would do all we could to improve our breeding stock as soon as we learned how to do so with regard to subluxation, but we weren't going to destroy all the fine things we had worked so hard to produce. It occurred to us that it might be that our dogs did not show the same amount of lameness that other dogs did because they worked harder and developed good muscles.

I talked with physiologists, who agreed with this theory. They told me the skeleton is held in shape by the muscles, not the muscles by the skeleton. I discussed this with veterinarians and got some support. I went to Davis and talked with Drs. Ghery D. Pettit and T. J. Hage. They felt that there was merit to the idea. Then we started to work with our 4-H puppy raisers. If one reported that a puppy was lame, we showed them how to lead it on a very tight lead so that it had to push hard with its hind feet. We had them start walking the puppy this way for a block and back, and building up to a half-mile a day, walking as fast as the child could walk.

We have not put a puppy to sleep for lameness in two years. In all but one of about a dozen and a half cases during that time, every puppy responded so well that lameness disappeared entirely, the dog was successfully trained as a Guide Dog, and is now doing excellent service. The idea is to build up the muscle tone so that the ball is pushed into the socket and kept there. At that age the whole formation seems to adjust, because calcification has not yet set in.

Ardith, a golden retriever from parents with good hips, became so lame that she could not get up alone. Ten-year-old Christine Stanley, 4-H Club puppy raiser, Westley, California, followed our instructions, lifting the pup to her feet to get her started. The X-rays at five months and a year were a revelation.

Dr. Pettit has approved this quotation from a valuable article by him in *PURE-BRED DOGS*, February, 1961: "The inheritance pattern of hip dysplasia is complex. . . . Regardless of the genetic terminology which applies, however, one should remember that hip structure is influenced by a complex gene pattern. The entire story is not yet known, but it should be apparent that any genetic study must be evaluated in the light of the author's definition of 'normal.' It has been shown that it is possible to reduce the incidence of hip dysplasia in a kennel by gradual selective breeding."

This is not one of the research fields for which our funds are allocated. Guide Dogs is carrying on with the help of Dr. Hage, who has received a grant at the University of California's College of Veterinary Medicine which will allow him to take more X-rays of the puppies, starting at four weeks of age, of our dogs when they enter training, and after four or five months of hard physical labor pulling on the Guide Dog harness. Dr. Hage's evaluation of the X-rays of our breeding stock enables us to avoid mating two dogs with the same faults. What is inherited and how it is inherited is a vital part of our program, whether the trait be physical or mental.

We have established that the "fetch trait" is inherited. At first it looked as though it were a true Mendelian inheritance, but further study showed it to be a complex inheritance. To us it has proven to be valuable because it indicates that a puppy likes to do something for its handler. We need to know more about this. We have established that when a dominant sire like Frank of Ledge Acres was inbred to his daughters or granddaughters, his influence for good was greater than when he was just the sire. Frankie has been dead several years. We have kept the descendants line-bred from him. We need to learn now if we have retained what Frankie gave us as a sire. If we have, then a breeder can hoard the fine qualities of great dogs in their progeny indefinitely, and perpetuate these great qualities almost exactly as they originally existed.

Another field in which we are especially interested is that of the critical periods so well established by Dr. Scott. It has been my experience that puppies weaned between twenty-one and twenty-eight days of age never adjust to conditions where they have to show initiative. They are also not very adaptable for work with other dogs. They do make fine pets. We need more data on this.

Physical, mental and emotional developments are of course affected by environment, but the knowledge about critical periods helps us to understand when environment has an effect upon a puppy. It is the key to when environment may be used most effectively, and when it has little or no effect. For this reason a more detailed study of the physical development of dogs is needed.

One measure of nervous development is the heart rate. Dr. Scott found that, "The heart is actually a very sensitive indicator of both body activity and various kinds of emotions. As will be

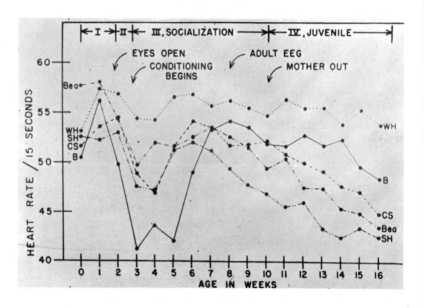

Bea = beagle
Wh = wire fox terrier
Sh = Shetland sheepdog
Cs = cocker spaniel
B = basenji

I II III IV at top designates the
critical period in life of the puppy.

seen on the graph (Figure 1.), the heart rate of the newborn puppy is very high and stays this way through the second week. Then it takes a very decided dip at from three to six weeks, coming back up to an earlier level around seven weeks of age. Thereafter, the heart rate slowly declines toward the adult level. These general changes seem to be independent of the breed. The first change occurs at the beginning of socialization, and its end occurs at seven weeks, coinciding approximately with the time of the adult EEG. We can suppose that this is the period when the complete cortical connections are established with the hypothalamus. We can conclude that the period from three to seven weeks is an especially sensitive one for emotional reaction, which corresponds to observation of overt behavior. We might also speculate that, since the cortex is not completely developed, emotional reactions during this time might be less permanently learned. On the other hand, they might be more disturbing because complete cortical control has not been established. We have here a fascinating field for further precise experiments on the effects of early experience." The foregoing is taken from *Psychosomatic Medicine*, Vol XX, No. 1, January-February, 1958, by permission of the author and publisher.

It is interesting to notice how the various breeds all show the same emotional disturbance at three weeks of age. What has happened in figure one is that each puppy was picked up and held for a minute while its heart rate was recorded. Actually this is no new experience, because each puppy is picked up and held while his heart rate is recorded six days a week from birth to sixteen weeks of age. At three weeks of age the puppy first senses that something is happening to it. If a puppy is weaned at this age it will not have had any consciousness of its litter mates or have experienced the love and discipline of its mother. To live a normal life in a world where there are other dogs, the puppy is better fitted for the experience if it lives from the age of three weeks to seven weeks with its mother and litter mates to become socialized.

This chart has a special significance to me. We have found that all breeds studied have almost identical critical periods. We see here the inherited traits of each breed showing up in the rate of his heart beats. Notice that the beagles, wire hairs, Shetlands, cockers and basenjis are all affected, but each in his own way and to his own degree. The beagle's heart rate starts the highest, but at sixteen weeks of age ends up next to the lowest, while the basenji starts lowest and ends up next to the highest.

There are so many things for us to explore: (1) We have never been able to train successfully for a Guide Dog a puppy who had been raised with her mother. (2) When two 4-H children in the same home raise two puppies from the same litter, one can always be trained, but never both. (3) We had a hundred per cent litter of Chesapeake Bay retrievers, eight in the litter, all trained perfectly for Guide Dogs. The next year the same parents produced a litter of sixteen. The mother died when the puppies were born and Mr. and Mrs. Johns raised them on bottles in their own home. At seven weeks of age they were transferred to the kennel. They tested as well as their brothers and sisters of the one hundred per cent litter. Twelve were trained—only one made a Guide Dog. All showed great emotional instability in training, although none had shown it in either Mr. Johns' home or in the 4-H homes. Most of them became dangerously aggressive as soon as they were put in training, yet they had had the kindest human care and attention. There were four adult dogs in the home of Mr. and Mrs. Johns with which they had had canine socialization, but they had not experienced canine mother love and discipline. Does a puppy have to have its own mother to rear it successfully to be emotionally sound? Would another dog as foster mother have made any difference?

Most of our active Guide Dogs live to be actively useful to their blind masters until they are ten years old; some go on for two or three years longer than that. This is often true of hunting dogs and herding dogs. Is useful employment a factor in longer life?

We find that most blind people change their attitude toward life for the better soon after they start training with a Guide Dog. What takes place in their outlook? Is the companionship of the dog partly responsible for this improvement or is it all in their emancipation?

There is so much about dogs to learn. There is also much about people to be learned, by studying dogs.

CHAPTER XVI

Subluxation Is Inherited

A trend which holds some promise of eventually eliminating complete luxation and subluxation due to congenital hip dysplasia, in dogs, has definitely been established in a study carried on by Guide Dogs for the Blind, Inc., in cooperation with the School of Veterinary Medicine, University of California, Davis, California.

By use of pelvic radiographs more than 100 of the breeding stock have been rated from 0 to 5. If one or both hips are completely luxated they are rated 0; subluxation of one or both hips 1; very shallow acetabula, or shallow acetabula with coxa valga, which means the internal angle of the femoral neck to the femoral shaft is more than 140° 2; fairly normal acetabula with coxa valga 3; fairly normal acetabula or a mild degree of coxa valga 4; normal acetabula and no coxa valga 5.

We have found that by mating dogs which are rated 3 to dogs with a 4 or 5 rating no puppies have ever been produced with luxations or subluxations. None of these categories have yet been developed to breed true, that is producing all puppies rating 4 or 5 from matings of dogs with these scores, but none of the puppies have rated less than 3.

Naturally we would not have bred any of the 1's and 2's had we known they were subluxated at the time, but the fact that we did have a few in our breeding stock has given us controls

203

which are very valuable in the study. We have also found that when these subluxated animals are mated to animals with a 4 or 5 rating, some of the offspring have had hips which were rated 4 or 5. This seems to indicate that some upgrading may be possible.

At present all puppies are X-rayed at 4 weeks of age and the dogs again at 12 months. In a year or two we should have very positive information and be able to state if the present trend is in fact a rule that can be depended upon.

The evaluation has been done by Dr. T. J. Hage, Associate Professor of Veterinary Medicine at Davis. The data analysis has been done by our Consulting Scientists, Dr. Benson Ginsburg, Professor of Biology, University of Chicago, and Mr. Sherman Bielfelt, Science Research Assistant on our project.

This statement has been read by and approved by

_____
T. J. Hage, Doctor Veterinary Medicine

_____
Benson Ginsburg, Professor Biology

As is customary in all our research when a trend is found by one of us, other members of our team double check our results. In this case, Dr. John L. Fuller, who is a physiologist associated with Dr. Hage in the subluxation study, picked up with Mr. Bielfelt where Drs. Hage and Ginsburg had left off and did a complete analysis of all the data we had which had been evaluated by Dr. Hage. Using the data available seems to indicate that both the trend is definite as far as our stock is concerned and, despite the fact that all progeny who showed any signs of lameness during the last two years have been X-rayed and their records included in the evaluation here, which would weight the study on the side of subluxation, the results are very promising.

Also it is interesting to note that the German shepherds who have been selectively line-bred longest and the Labradors which were started to be selective-bred before the Golden retrievers, were rated higher, respective to the sequence of selective line-breeding.

A preliminary analysis of the inheritance of hip dysplasia has been made using ratings and diagnoses prepared by Dr. T. J. Hage of the University of California at Davis. Three classes of individuals were recognized; poor (some subluxation—rated 0 or 1 on the Hage scale); fair (some defect in structure or low grade arthritis—rated 2 or 3 on the Hage scale). The third class of individuals is near perfect (5 rates better musculature than 4 on the Hage scale.) We had 98 progeny from 39 matings for which ratings were available on both sire and dam.

The heritability of good hip structure is well illustrated by the data. When sires with good hips are mated with good or fair dams, no poor hips were observed in 37 progeny. When "fair" sires were used, 10 out of 56 (18%) were rated as poor. None of the group breed true. A hypothesis of multiple factor inheritance is in agreement with the data.

It should be emphasized that the sample studied is small and is not representative of dogs in general or even of the complete Guide Dog stock. Only recently have X-rays been made on all subjects. An animal which goes lame is more apt to be included in the sample; hence the prevalence of dysplasia is probably overestimated. With these reservations in mind it is of interest to note that the average ratings on the Hage scale for the three chief breeds in the Guide Dogs stock were: German shepherds, 3.18; Labradors, 2.78; Goldens, 2.68, based on 0 to 5 rating scale.

Hip dysplasia results from a poor fit between the thigh and hip bone. It appears, as Dr. Ginsburg has stated, that the form of these two bones is inherited independently, and that there is a third factor in subluxation—the mass and strength of the hip musculature. A genetic analysis based upon measurement of individual parts of the hips may be more instructive than one based upon a rating scale which attempts to average a large number of independent variables.

Addenda

I am immensely grateful to so many people who have made contributions to this book in one way or another, but who have gone unmentioned here. There are, however, a few who must be mentioned before I sign off. Please, will all the rest of you just accept my thanks.

Mr. and Mrs. Harold Glidden, Presque Isle, Maine, have constantly been a source of encouragement. They have done so many nice things, such as finding us the Hamor Cottage on Frenchman's Bay in which we enjoyed two summers and an autumn. They provided me with the hunting lodge on Hobart Hill, where I wrote the original ten chapters which appeared in *Pure Bred Dogs*; they also provided me with a car so I could cruise back and forth between Hobart Hill and Bar Harbor for consultations with Drs. Scott and Fuller while doing the articles. Their delightful home in Presque Isle has long been one of our favorite places.

I must also thank another one of Juanita's cousins, Irving Glidden, and his wife. They took me on my first trip to Bar Harbor by auto, driving most of one night going, and another coming home. It was just after the war. The roads were bad and cars were all badly worn and parts hard to come by. Most of us hesitated about giving our old cars a workout like that. Thanks again.

Near Bar Harbor, at Hulls Cove, Dr. and Mrs. John L. Fuller opened their lovely, big, colonial home to Juanita and me on the Bar Harbor ends of our safaris. Not only did they provide a lovely home away from home, but gave constant help and encouragement with my book.

I think it is interesting to know that the father of General Pierpont Morgan Hamilton gave Hamilton Station to the Roscoe B. Jackson Memorial Laboratory, because now his daughter-in-law is president of Guide Dogs for the Blind, and devotes most of her time to making the service of this organization the finest in the world for those who need dogs to lead them. Both Mrs. Hamilton and General Hamilton are most ardent workers for the cause, and highly appreciate the fine dogs.

BIBLIOGRAPHY

ALL OWNERS of pure-bred dogs will benefit themselves and their dogs by enriching the knowledge of breeds and of canine care, training, breeding, psychology and other important aspec of dog management. The following list of books covers further reading recommended by judge veterinarians, breeders, trainers and other authorities. Books may be obtained at the finer bo stores and pet shops, or through Howell Book House Inc., publishers, New York.

Breed Books

AFGHAN HOUND, Complete — Miller & Gilbert
AIREDALE, New Complete — Edwards
AKITA, Complete — Linderman & Funk
ALASKAN MALAMUTE, Complete — Riddle & Seeley
BASSET HOUND, Complete — Braun
BEAGLE, New Complete — Noted Authorities
BLOODHOUND, Complete — Brey & Reed
BOXER, Complete — Denlinger
BRITTANY SPANIEL, Complete — Riddle
BULLDOG, New Complete — Hanes
BULL TERRIER, New Complete — Eberhard
CAIRN TERRIER, Complete — Marvin
CHESAPEAKE BAY RETRIEVER, Complete — Cherry
CHIHUAHUA, Complete — Noted Authorities
COCKER SPANIEL, New — Kraeuchi
COLLIE, New — Official Publication of the Collie Club of America
DACHSHUND, The New — Meistrell
DALMATIAN, The — Treen
DOBERMAN PINSCHER, New — Walker
ENGLISH SETTER, New Complete — Tuck, Howell & Graef
ENGLISH SPRINGER SPANIEL, New — Goodall & Gasow
FOX TERRIER, New Complete — Silvernail
GERMAN SHEPHERD DOG, New Complete — Bennett
GERMAN SHORTHAIRED POINTER, New — Maxwell
GOLDEN RETRIEVER, New Complete — Fischer
GORDON SETTER, Complete — Look
GREAT DANE, New Complete — Noted Authorities
GREAT DANE, The—Dogdom's Apollo — Draper
GREAT PYRENEES, Complete — Strang & Giffin
IRISH SETTER, New Complete — Eldredge & Vanacore
IRISH WOLFHOUND, Complete — Starbuck
JACK RUSSEL TERRIER, Complete — Plummer
KEESHOND, Complete — Peterson
LABRADOR RETRIEVER, Complete — Warwick
LHASA APSO, Complete — Herbel
MINIATURE SCHNAUZER, Complete — Eskrigge
NEWFOUNDLAND, New Complete — Chern
NORWEGIAN ELKHOUND, New Complete — Wallo
OLD ENGLISH SHEEPDOG, Complete — Mandeville
PEKINGESE, Quigley Book of — Quigley
PEMBROKE WELSH CORGI, Complete — Sargent & Harper
POODLE, New Complete — Hopkins & Irick
POODLE CLIPPING AND GROOMING BOOK, Complete — Kalstone
ROTTWEILER, Complete — Freeman
SAMOYED, Complete — Ward
SCHIPPERKE, Official Book of — Root, Martin, Kent
SCOTTISH TERRIER, New Complete — Marvin
SHETLAND SHEEPDOG, The New — Riddle
SHIH TZU, Joy of Owning — Seranne
SHIH TZU, The (English) — Dadds
SIBERIAN HUSKY, Complete — Demidoff
TERRIERS, The Book of All — Marvin
WEST HIGHLAND WHITE TERRIER, Complete — Marvin
WHIPPET, Complete — Pegram
YORKSHIRE TERRIER, Complete — Gordon & Bennett

Breeding

ART OF BREEDING BETTER DOGS, New — Onstott
BREEDING YOUR OWN SHOW DOG — Seranne
HOW TO BREED DOGS — Whitney
HOW PUPPIES ARE BORN — Prine
INHERITANCE OF COAT COLOR IN DOGS — Little

Care and Training

COUNSELING DOG OWNERS, Evans Guide for — Eva
DOG OBEDIENCE, Complete Book of — Saunde
NOVICE, OPEN AND UTILITY COURSES — Saunde
DOG CARE AND TRAINING FOR BOYS AND GIRLS — Saunde
DOG NUTRITION, Collins Guide to — Colli
DOG TRAINING FOR KIDS — Benjam
DOG TRAINING, Koehler Method of — Koehl
DOG TRAINING Made Easy — Tuck
GO FIND! Training Your Dog to Track — Dav
GUARD DOG TRAINING, Koehler Method of — Koehl
MOTHER KNOWS BEST—The Natural Way to Train Your Dog — Benjam
OPEN OBEDIENCE FOR RING, HOME AND FIELD, Koehler Method of — Koeh
STONE GUIDE TO DOG GROOMING FOR ALL BREEDS — Sto
SUCCESSFUL DOG TRAINING, The Pearsall Guide to — Pears
TOY DOGS, Kalstone Guide to Grooming All — Kalsto
TRAINING THE RETRIEVER — Kersl
TRAINING TRACKING DOGS, Koehler Method of — Koehl
TRAINING YOUR DOG—Step by Step Manual — Volhard & Fish
TRAINING YOUR DOG TO WIN OBEDIENCE TITLES — Mors
TRAIN YOUR OWN GUN DOG, How to — Good
UTILITY DOG TRAINING, Koehler Method of — Koeh
VETERINARY HANDBOOK, Dog Owner's Home — Carlson & Gif

General

AKC'S WORLD OF THE PURE-BRED DOG — American Kennel Cl
CANINE TERMINOLOGY — Sp
COMPLETE DOG BOOK, The — Official Publication American Kennel Cl
DOG IN ACTION, The — Ly
DOG BEHAVIOR, New Knowledge of — Pfaffenberg
DOG JUDGE'S HANDBOOK — Tietj
DOG JUDGING, Nicholas Guide to — Nichol
DOG PEOPLE ARE CRAZY — Ridc
DOG PSYCHOLOGY — Whitn
DOGSTEPS, Illustrated Gait at a Glance — Ellic
DOG TRICKS — Haggerty & Benjam
ENCYCLOPEDIA OF DOGS, International — Dangerfield, Howell & Ridc
EYES THAT LEAD—Story of Guide Dogs for the Blind — Tuck
FRIEND TO FRIEND—Dogs That Help Mankind — Schwa
FROM RICHES TO BITCHES — Shattuc
HAPPY DOG/HAPPY OWNER — Sieg
IN STITCHES OVER BITCHES — Shattuc
JUNIOR SHOWMANSHIP HANDBOOK — Brown & Mas
MY TIMES WITH DOGS — Fletch
OUR PUPPY'S BABY BOOK (blue or pink)
SUCCESSFUL DOG SHOWING, Forsyth Guide to — Forsy
TRIM, GROOM & SHOW YOUR DOG, How to — Saunde
WHY DOES YOUR DOG DO THAT? — Bergm
WILD DOGS in Life and Legend — Ridc
WORLD OF SLED DOGS, From Siberia to Sport Racing — Copping